SHEDDING SHAME AND CLAIMING FREEDOM

CLAIMING FREEDOM

How to Eradicate Our Most Painful Emotion

Anne Stirling Hastings

Acknowledgements

Elizabeth Wedington, Elif Beall and Kelly Monjazeb contributed thinking regarding shame and it's healing. Connie Lakowski gave honest feedback. L J Lumpkin and Nana Morris offered support. I appreciate all of you!

CONTENTS

Introduction

Humanness brings with it the right to belong in a community and develop ourselves to the fullest. No one is on the outside. Shame can interfere with knowing this. The person who feels unworthy will feel as if they are not entitled to belong.

You know what shame feels like, that hot face, skin crawling sensation that makes you want to be anywhere else. The intense wanting to make the other person wrong, to affirm that they are wrong about you. And those bad feelings you have about yourself, that you don't deserve self care, perhaps even being alive. The embarrassment when you make a mistake, when you did something you feel is wrong. Those secrets that you don't want anyone to know about you. The sick, shaky feeling of being found out. Losing when compared with others regarding money, work, education, and looks. The desire to be seen as a good person even though feeling like you don't deserve self-esteem.

Then there are the many ways you avoid feeling it. Drinking, working too much, being busy, talking on and on, achieving in order to prove yourself, addictions, and the big one – shaming others. Criticizing others, gossiping, looking down on. People who buy what they can't afford, or gamble compulsively, or shop addictively, or focus on wanting what they can't have are suffering from shame that prevents understanding that we all deserve true belonging.

This emotion distorts us so much that it brings about a long list of personal and social distortions. Hatred, revenge, racism, sexism, addictions, rape, child molestation, child abuse, cruelty, economic recessions, parenting difficulties, lying, employment conflicts, marital problems, most mental illness, and absurd reasoning by banks and stock purchasers based on greed, are caused by shame. They are all caused by our loving humanness interrupted by shame followed by countless methods of avoiding shame, resulting in the blind harming of every one of us. Shame is the underlying culprit that has to be healed in order for everything else to work well. World peace cannot be obtained by political changes. It will only come when each one of us takes on the task of finding our integrity, and the painful healing of shame to obtain it.

Healing shame requires
facing shame.

I am purifying myself of shame in order to become more fully human. I have progressively given up culturally prescribed methods of feeling connected. I used work and parenting and social drinking and relationships and projects and sports and countless small methods to avoid knowing how little connection I had. Finally, as I gave these up, I saw that not a single person is capable of continuous intimacy with no need for defensive maneuvers.

Discharging shame and fear brings love and contentment and intimacy. Any fears I had about not fitting in, losing friends and relatives, feeling alone and isolated, and preferring to be dead than live the life I had, were not founded in reality! When I hear friends and clients express these fears, I nod, because I once had them! Instead of things being worse, I have the love that is available. I belong in the whole world. I can embrace all my arenas of life. And I don't yearn for someone or something to make things better.

Healing

I learned how to heal shame as a psychologist seeing clients, and addressing mine. I have included my story and others' to show how shame becomes attached to each of us, and how to remove it.

I have spent most of my life healing. Picture memory, emotional memory and body memory indicate severe emotional, sexual and physical abuse when I was very young. I was chronically depressed throughout childhood and early adult life, alternating with occasional pleasant life experiences. Before I was born my mother believed I had unusual powers, and she needed to make sure I used them for good instead of evil. She gave up, however, and viewed me as some strange alien, an identity I adopted. I developed what attachment theory calls avoidant attachment, living isolated and separate from the family and community. I couldn't I fit in and belong. When I tell the experiences of my young life it comes across as if no one else had been there.

Shame and fear and depression prevented me from using my intelligence, and from being curious. Fantasy took up all my time. I did poorly in school, barely got into college, and didn't begin excelling until half way through. Once away from home I made friends and for the first time, had a community. I began to enjoy school, discovering what I liked.

When my son was born I fell into an intense, agitated depression, later learning how giving birth brings up abuses from childhood. I went into therapy and learned how one's history causes symptoms, and how we project childhood relationships onto the present, believing they are still true. I cried and talked in psychoanalysis, which helped, but back in the 70's trauma healing wasn't understood. Self-help books had not yet made it to the market.

I had "avoidantly attached" as an attempt to not believe my mother's view of me as evil. Yet I became heavily shame-based just from my unacceptability to her. My defenses against this emotional abuse were strong, but were unable to entirely shield me from her deeply held conviction of my horribleness. While other children develop active lives to offset their shame, I fell into depression. I felt as if I had no life. When I was old enough to discover fantasy I imagined a future life, when I would be grown up. That was my best defense. But it was only a coping tool. It didn't change my internalized shame.

While avoidant attachment separated me from others, and prevented belonging, it had certain advantages. I could think for myself, learn how to heal, and create a career. I was so outside the social norm that operating out of it was normal. Even though my parents valued education, they reacted no differently to my poor grades in high school than they did to my getting a doctorate. I was an enigmatic alien. They didn't know what to make of me.

Embracing a freedom that most people don't have allowed me to develop a practice that I call Following My Feet. This phrase arrived when I discovered the pleasure of going where my feet went on exercise walks with no plan about where, or how fast, or how long or how far. I had already come to respect that I lived according to my intuitive understanding of what was needed next. Being an alien, I didn't have to consider what was expected of me in this culture or by my family. Anything I did was no surprise to them.

Foot Following sounds like such a good thing, and actually it is, but it wasn't a source of safety as having a mentor would have been. Instead, I was alone. But Feet keep me pressed against the next difficult healing task.

The emotional healing that began when my son was born occurs in bouts. My life goes along seemingly normal for a while, and then some piece of traumatic memory leaps up for attention. Long ago I didn't understand why bad dreams, feeling horrible on awakening, or finding myself disoriented and spacey for most of a day was actually the re-experience of something that happened long ago. Now I set out to process each new piece.

The themes of love and support and connection and community ran through my life and my work. As people get better in therapy they are more capable of accepting themselves, and then of loving openly and with satisfaction. I could see that there is no shortcut to love. "Falling in love" doesn't bring love, it brings sexual bonding and a sense of permanence, along with temporary approval and adoration. This brings shame to a halt. For a while. Deciding to love doesn't bring it about either. I came to see that our particular defenses against pain, and our projections of past relationships onto present ones, inhibit the exchange of love. These have to be healed in order to have the natural human experience of loving and receiving love.

I saw how I had attempted to ameliorate shame as an approach to getting better, and how that really didn't help. The shame was still showing up in dreams. Some people seem to be able to avoid their shame to enjoy their lives and not need to heal it. I am not one of them.

These fears, however, have alerted me to one of the reasons to join a group of people. Belonging to a healing sub-culture provides connection until we reach the place of knowing we are never alone.

Feet finally let me see the big picture. I have the skills, and I know how to remove the obstacles!

The distortion begins when we are conceived into existence and are not given what we truly need. We can't take our place. We can't see what is natural and correct, we lose perception of our instincts. We can no longer automatically respond to the emotional signals, like birds always looking for predators, and cats alerted by unfamiliar noises, and babies crying desperately when left with a sitter.

Used well, religion, self-help programs, psycho-therapy, meditation, spiritual practices, or taking care of one's home, yard, and family could lead us back to the shame-free existence and our place in the natural order of things.

I couldn't understand, or see, the big picture of existence until I had sufficiently healed shame. I repaired most of the effects of having been deprived of essential mothering when I was conceived and born. I am filling up the empty spot within. I belong in the world no matter how distorted all those around me are.

Chapter 1: Shame: The Basics

What Is Shame?

Most simply, shame is a terribly unpleasant emotion. Healthy shame is a gentle alert that tells us we would be happier if we shifted gears. Toxic shame, a term offered by John Bradshaw in his best seller, *Healing the Shame That Binds You* (2005), is that dreadful, self-directed sense of badness. It can include feeling pointless and hopeless, deadened, with no reason to go on. It is the greatest enemy of living a rich, communal life.

Shame can be experienced in many ways including anxiety, depression, loneliness, yearning for love and contact, fear of being seen, and wanting evidence of success. It's a heaviness that separates one from other people, and from oneself. Apathy, lack of interest and lack of pleasure are signs that shame is making its way past the inhibitors.

Every single one of us carries shame. We believe that we are bad or harmful, and we try to figure out how to not be. If we are just good enough, or polite or helpful, then we can believe that we aren't bad after all.

Every one of us also uses methods to avoid feeling shame. We distract ourselves from it with alcohol, drugs and other addictive substances, and with addictive behaviors. Smart people use intellectual defenses of rationalizing, explaining, arguing and feeling always right.

The price for sidestepping the horror of shame is the loss of so much of our humanness. We have to be out of touch with love and connection and vulnerability in order to avoid the one feeling we don't want. When we release shame, we become increasingly able to claim the richness of life. You can begin with your actual experience of shame, or from the ways you try to stay away from it.

The barriers we create against
feeling shame prevent the
full experience of love and community.

Shame Harms

We have been shamed and brainwashed in ways that interfere with development of our human potential. We are left with figuring out how to develop our loving selves. If we didn't believe we were shameful we wouldn't need to be told what being good and being bad are. We would just know. We wouldn't need to learn how to pray, or to forgive, because these are automatically within us.

We have been harmed, and so we must heal. If we had not been harmed, we would have nothing to heal with religious and spiritual practice. We would not have to become "good."

Internalized Shame

Shame can become part of one's very identity. We believe it is who we are. My internalized shame came from my mother seeing me as unusually bad, more so than my innocent brother and sister. She communicated it with cold stares and a calm, hard voice. If I believed her, as children do, I would have felt so terrible that life would have seemed impossible to live. So I kept the shame outside of my soul by distancing myself from her, and then from everyone around me. Thus came my "avoidant attachment" style of relating.

Children receive shaming looks and comments and impatience. The negative impact of this would be less than when seen as evil because it is less shaming. The methods of defending against it would be smaller, too. My sister learned that if she were calm and good, our mother would be moderately critical, so she integrated these behaviors into her view of how she would be. Who she was, her identity.

My mother's behaviors year after year supported my understanding of her perception of me as evil. One obvious example is neglecting my need for braces until I was seventeen, and then only minimally because of leaving soon for college. Money was not an issue.

It didn't occur to me to ask for braces when I was twelve because I was an alien, and only human children had this right. Even when my mother mentioned that my friend worked to pay for her own braces, I didn't see myself as belonging in the same category.

It is startling to realize this truth. My parents were educated, my father a high status professional, we lived in a nice house, my mother stayed at home with the children, there were no divorces. These were the standards of respectability in my family. Yet inside that good presentation was the bizarre treatment of a child.

Healthy Shame

Bradshaw and others address what they call good shame in contrast to the toxic variety. Bradshaw sees shame as a motivator for humans to live good lives. I believe that we are born geared to have good lives, and so integrity is natural and desirable when we get shame out of the way. It is a positive draw. Good shame and good guilt assist us when we shift away from the natural positive draw. It says, "Nope! Stop. Go the other way." When obeyed, integrity feels really good - not because it turns off a painful signal but because of gaining access again to the positive signal.

Bradshaw and other writers see shame as an individual feeling, held within a single person. Therefore, individual change is needed. I see healthy shame as serving a community function.

Feeling badly for lying, stealing, abusing, killing, etc., supports the existence of well-working order. Healthy shame and guilt are our signals that we are not doing our part. Somehow this shame took on far greater meaning and impact over history, resulting in a belief in one's badness instead of using it as a signal of having done something harmful, and as a stimulus to right it. Healthy shame is mild and feels really good! It needs to be seen in contrast to the inhibiting, painful experience that results in so much harm in the world.

We have lost most of our community orientation, and so all we can see is ourselves. The well working community described in *The Continuum Concept*, by Jean Liedloff is fully supportive and integrated. Individuals don't sacrifice themselves or their uniqueness in order to belong to the larger group. Instead, they are able to be entirely themselves, meet their own needs and desires, and function fully in the service of the community.

Being fully oneself and
functioning fully in community
aren't incompatible!
This is how we are intended to live.

In a novel called *The Kin of Ata Are Waiting for You,* Dorothy Bryant describes a way of life that honors each person's unique contribution while, at the same time, community is central.

Healthy shame and integrity
pull us forward.
Toxic shame pushes us.

Toxic Shame

There are two kinds of toxic shame. One is internal, our own voices received from countless reflections of our badness. The other is shame when seen by others when we are doing something defined as shameful by the culture. These include being mean, unclothed, urinating or defecating, using bad table manners, being sexual and countless other acts.

The Shame System

When two or more people join together to shame and counter shame, or together shame others, or help each other avoid the feeling of shame we call it being in the shame system. When one person shames another, and the second shames back, circular arguing takes off. People are in the shame system when they join together to triangulate against, or gossip about, other people or institutions, or when rescuing each other from feeling shame, such as by joking about it. Our culture has complex rules about how shame systems work, which will be addressed throughout this book. This includes how we are to help each other not feel acculturated shame.

How Toxic Shame Plays Out in Everyday Life

Feeling like a bad, horrible, harmful person is perhaps the most obvious experience of shame. This includes low self-esteem, shyness, feeling awkward, self-criticism or a general feeling of hopelessness about life. Feeling unimportant to, or unloved by, spouses, friends, children and others. Thinking you are at fault if others have difficulty with what you do. You are not enough.

Fear of engendering feelings of shame prevents people from pursuing a life that is right for them. This includes looking for jobs, getting education or training, asking questions to find the right path, relating to possible love partners with ease and curiosity, and exploring satisfying places in which to live.

Fear of public speaking is based on the fear of shame. If there are no true dangers awaiting, then fear is irrational. Some aren't afraid of being shamed, but this is a good place to check when it shows up, because most fear is. Finding my heart rate increasing and my palms sweaty when standing on a cliff is from fear of heights. But the nervousness when giving a talk is from fear of feeling shame.

A woman explained in detail how it wasn't personal when she turned down my offer to play racquetball. She was trying to make sure I wouldn't feel shame at her refusal. She was avoiding feeling her own shame that would come from causing me to feel it. Avoiding shame causes so much wasted relating. We are compelled to learn how to avoid our own shame, and how to avoid "making" others feel it. Imagine how much energy and thought and creativity would be available to live fully if we didn't have to attend to this emotion!

Asking for a raise, for a promotion, for time off, for a change in duties can carry fear of disapproval. Disapproval isn't inherently harmful, but for those who depend on the perception of others to avoid feeling shame, it can feel very harmful.

The employer may feel uncomfortable saying no, and react with discomfort, perhaps wanting to shame the employee to avoid his own feelings. The shame goes around and around.

Being wrong in an argument, failing, letting people down, not seeing someone coming through the door, stepping on someone's foot, saying something objectionable: these are all experienced as worthy of shame. So are burping, farting, smelling bad, or having stains on clothes. When a champion athlete makes mistakes he is shamed by fans.

Being chosen last when players are selected is told as a horrible childhood experience. All it means is that they thought you weren't a good player. It has nothing to do with goodness or badness or the right to be alive. Failing in any way, including getting into college, getting degrees, getting jobs, getting dates, getting or accepting marriage proposals, investing well, have nothing to do with who we are as human beings worthy of life!

A boy about nine years old deliberately squeaked his shoes in Starbucks on his way to the bathroom. After they received their order he asked his mother if he could have some soy milk. She said no in a shaming tone. He obviously knew that he would receive that answer. That shaming.

Why do so many children do that? Clients have explained that their childhood treatment was so bad, they actually felt better when they brought on abuse instead of waiting for it. Perhaps that is what the boy was doing. Or maybe his identity had become shame-based. Then it can actually be more comfortable to act shame-worthy to avoid feeling shame than to try to be good and still be shamed.

My mother criticized me with words like cold, hard, cruel, unkind, thoughtless, unloving, and selfish. I thought I didn't believe her that I was evil, but I spent my life proving she was wrong. That was actually a kind of agreement that she was right. Occasionally I did things that I couldn't justify as not shame-worthy, and dropped into depression, thinking that I had no life. Without understanding, it was difficult to heal from my belief in my own shame. My conviction that all I had to do was prove I'm not bad set me up to continue feeling bad!

What about when a person does harmful things such as stealing, cheating, lying, manipulating, being unfaithful, hitting, abusing children, raping, or murdering? Healthy shame is an appropriate feeling because its purpose is to help that person stop the action from the inside out rather than from external controls. Intense toxic shame isn't helpful. It is actually the reason people do these harmful things. Toxic shame deprives them of healthy shame.

Lying and Cheating

I have worked with sex addicts and their spouses for many years, and have learned what goes on in the minds of men and women who have sex outside of their relationship, and then create a network of lies to hide it.

If you have done this, you know that it feels miserable. First something drives a person to seek sexual intrigue outside the marriage. Affairs, flirting, casual sex or Internet porn. The need to resort to this way of feeling enlivened is to avoid feeling shame. But it brings more shame. Then lying about it brings even more.

A client came to me because he read an article I wrote called "Cats Don't Lie." He saw in my bio that I see sex addicts. He was filled with shame over his infidelities and lying to his wife. He was greatly relieved that I didn't add more shame on to the pile, and that I focused on removing it. Sadly, he had been shamed by his wife for twenty-five years and with her voice etched into his brain, had a hard time believing me. He thought he deserved shaming.

Over time he was able to understand that relinquishing toxic shame would free up the more gentle, healthy kind. Then he could step out of his intellectual defenses and claim real emotions.

The culture believes that men who cheat and lie are cold and hard, calloused, without integrity. But the opposite can be true. The attempt to stop feeling their high level of shame in turn brings more. Then the impaired relating with his wife and everyone else makes him feel removed and separate. Men who begin healing their shame become able to experience intimacy.

While it is obvious that countless people have no access to conscience, and others commit crimes in order to belong, most lying and cheating is the result of toxic shame.

My cats, don't feel shame for anything. I love that. They also don't shame me! They may ask for what they want, even demand it, even getting angry when I don't provide it. But they don't think I am a bad person worthy of condemnation!

Our culture believes that
anger is harmful because
the object of the anger feels shame.

When anger is expressed in a shaming, critical manner, it isn't truly an expression of anger. True anger is a natural emotion that can cleanse many kinds of distress. A vital component of grief, it functions to leave the past in the past so we can claim the present. It is an energizing, boundary-setting emotion. However, this true anger has been maligned by a shame-ridden culture, and is now seen as harmful.

Gossip

Gossip is the triangulating or joining of the good people against the bad or stupid or ugly ones. No one likes to be the subject of gossip. Why is that? It isn't pleasant, of course, but if we didn't carry our own internalized shame, we could simply know that these people aren't communing friends, and let it go. We would have the freedom to see the truth.

"What will the neighbors think?" This makes us manipulate the neighbors' perception of us. In other words, deceive them. When we stop wearing the right clothes, buying the right car, smiling at the right times, we will indeed be the subject of gossip. Others will shame us. But they are anyway! No one is free from the shaming of others. We are too rich or too poor, dressed too well or not well enough. Something can always be found wrong with any one of us.

Again at Starbucks, I sat near a woman who seemed uncomfortable with my being there. I thought I might be too close for her comfort. After five minutes her friend arrived. She then asked me if she could remove her magazine from under my napkin, letting me guess that she had been trying to save my chair for her friend. I said I could move so her friend could sit there, and she thanked me profusely. Why couldn't she tell me she was saving the chair? Why did she need to thank me over and over? Why did moving have to be my idea? It was all shame, fear that I would provoke her internalized shame from the past. If she had been able to tell me, I would have said, yes, I'm glad to. Look at the stress she went through because shame prevented her from saying what she needed, and working with me to get it.

Shame is also called embarrassment, that feeling when someone comes to the door when you're in your bathrobe. Or when you don't hear what the person says and give the wrong answer. When your children make too much noise in stores.

Getting Out of the Shame System

At a family visit I became aware of a shaming interaction, and by becoming aware, was able to step out of the shame system and the automatic response. During conversation, my son mentioned that someone had graduated from a particular high school, and when I asked where that was, he looked at me shamingly. It was his own high school. His father, sitting next to him, gave me the same look. Their faces were contorted into the frown and mouth-clenching that communicates astonishment that a person could be so stupid-cruel-selfish-hurtful-thoughtless-unloving. My daughter-in-law scolded me, but in a humorous style that offered me a way out. I was to say, yeah, aren't I awful? And laugh with her.

However, because of shame healing, I am different. In the past I would have said, "Well, what can I say!" and made some joke about being senile. By doing so, I would have entered the shame system. Instead, I simply said "It is a memory issue." The shaming from the men continued. I sat still, looking at them, and really saw. I wanted to cry. I was being attacked even while they wouldn't think they were attacking.

I didn't feel shame. I never would have in this situation. But in the past I would have avoided seeing how I was being shamed because I would have joined in the shame system. I could have said, "Well, I guess I'm just an idiot!," or challenged them with knowing the name of my high school, or stated that my brain is so full of Important learning that I let the insignificant details slip out, or said what's the big deal about remembering the name of a high school. This would have been met with further comments, possibly referring to my lack of caring, or lack of intelligence, or it might have been done with looks and sounds.

I used to use these maneuvers even though I didn't believe the statements. By joining in the shame system, I wouldn't have even seen how their faces were so contorted into expressing hateful condemnation. I didn't see! And then I didn't have to react. But now that I was looking, and not responding in the system, I was able to see the degree to which harsh, mean, condemning treatment is doled out in the name of humor. I could also see that they didn't know they were shaming me.

If shaming weren't integrated into the culture, these men would have reflected on my poor memory. They would have seen that I don't remember names well even though I am intelligent. They would have reminded me in a matter-of-fact tone that this was my son's high school. The way this was handled demonstrates how there is no intimacy and compassion and caring and love and witnessing possible when playing in the shaming system. And, need I even say this, there is no communing.

As I thought about my visit, I realized that seeing the shaming is more painful than responding in the system and not seeing it! Seeing shaming sets me apart. I am separate from these people. At the very same time, it allows me to heal from receiving shame, and from engaging in a false, harmful system. Apparently I had to be far enough along in healing from being told I was evil to be able to see clearly. I am strong enough to see the shaming, and to not take it on. It also requires strength to see how damaging these behaviors are to others, too. How everyone harms everyone all around them in an attempt to not feel shame-worthy. Yet these very acts of shaming others have to heap more shame on the shamers.

Even though I was astonished at seeing shaming directed at me, I appreciate being able to see the level of shame carried by others. Why would this family find it enlivening to humorously shame each other for hours at a time? They engage in competitive shaming in a manner well within the culture.

When I was in my 30's and early 40's I enjoyed shaming those who I thought deserved it. The president of a company pursuing my then-husband for employment was drunk and set out to establish that he could win a verbal encounter with me. I turned it back on him, putting him in the one-down position, getting the other execs and wives to laugh at him. I really enjoyed this. He set up the competition and I won.

Now I would find it satisfying to not engage. If he pursued, as he probably would after drinking all day at a ballgame, followed by a long period in the bar before dinner, I could have described what he was doing. Or I might have said nothing, just looked at him. My eyes and those of the others would have reflected himself back to him. I can still take charge, and feel personally powerful, but now in an entirely different manner. It might have saved him from being the butt of jokes at the office the next day.

In order to not engage in his competition, I would have had to see what was going on. This is what has changed. My years of studying people in my office and in the world has educated me about the mental illness – which is really shame and the methods to avoid feeling it - that forces people to treat each other meanly. From this place of seeing, I can sidestep meanness. I find it no longer interesting to give out, either.

People who cling to a victim stance use shaming others as a way to prevent feeling their own shame. A man explained to me how he had registered with the Do Not Call Registry, and when receiving a solicitation, asked for the name and number of the person. With great pleasure he informed her that he was going to report her. He enjoyed getting one over on another, and again in the telling. I was invited to share my own examples.

A great deal of time and social interaction is spent telling stories that have to do with shame. Shaming others, our own feeling of being shamed, winning over someone who is doing wrong, differentiating the good people from the bad people.

A friend who heard me talk about shame told me how her new awareness was helping. Someone called her mid-morning when she was still sleeping. Her friend said, "Shame on you for sleeping late!" Immediately she heard the word shame! We realized that her friend wasn't trying to shame her, she was responding out of cultural habit. My friend added that this phrase was backed up by the whole culture!

Teasing children "playfully" can be shaming. At the beach, a little girl in bare feet asked her father in a whiny voice to carry her back to the car. He said playfully, "What, you want me to carry you? You're heavy!" She said, "I'm not heavy." He replied, "Yes, you are, you're a big girl," all in a playfully shaming tone. He seems to be a sweet father, but he is conveying that she is wrong to ask to be carried, that it is an imposition. Instead he could have gently explained that he isn't strong enough to carry her that far, and that she would have to walk.

Status

Acculturated shame conveys that the status of jobs and wealth and education means that some people are worth more than others. They are higher on the ladder. Barack Obama's inaugural speech fluidly reached out to us as a community, preparing to work with us to undo the damage to our economy. But when newscasters spoke of him, they included the high level of his and Michele's education, supporting the belief that they are superior to the masses.

Instead we could all be glad that they found right ways to use their intelligence and interests, and that those ways support our needs for governing, our needs for community. It doesn't make them more worthy human beings.

Instead of lauding people who are wealthy or educated, and by default putting down those who aren't, a healthy culture would support all people in discovering the right way for each to live, for each to develop gifts and interests. Then all of us could best support individuals and community. No job would be valued over any other job. Valuing would depend on the personality of each person, and what the job means to them.

Depression and Anxiety

Depression and anxiety are seen as mental symptoms and addressed by therapy and pharmaceuticals. Therapists can help relieve these symptoms by changing beliefs that bring them on, or by assisting with grief for past traumas. However, the underlying cause of depression, anxiety and panic is shame.

Many clients will understand that the source of their feelings of self hate need to be addressed. These include abuse - physical, emotional and sexual. They also include shame-filled marriages. Symptoms arise because methods used to diminish this shame aren't working.

*Healing internalized shame will
heal depression and anxiety.*

I was seriously depressed in my early life, and it didn't abate until I had been in therapy for some time. Back in the '70's the primary benefit from talking and crying every week was being listened to, having my needs taken seriously, and feeling cared for. I saw this therapist as a third parent, as it was clear that much of what I received had not been available when I was growing up. This kind person who took me seriously gave me something that countered the beliefs I had developed from being raised by a hating mother. I had an emotional experience of the truth - my mother was wrong. I wasn't evil. I was capable of being a good mother and a loving person.

Since my depression came in part from negative feelings about myself, sitting across from someone who didn't agree with that assessment was powerful. The internalized shame from my mother's views was replaced by self-acceptance which became possible from having a valid reflection of who I am. My therapist saw me as loving, competent, intelligent, and with a right to be in the world. He didn't think I was an alien. While no one else thought I was, either, my style of relating at a distance kept me from taking in the views of others. It took intense sessions for me to let down my guard and actually grasp that I was seen, and that what was seen was not an evil alien.

The depression lifted, I went to graduate school, and started discovering many ways to heal. As I learned to help others, I learned how to help myself.

How Shame Was Placed on Us

Head-shaking, eye-rolling, criticism, name-calling, saying "How could you have done that?" or "What were you thinking?" "You can't live like that!" Impatient tones and annoyance are usually shaming. When my son was a young child, I spoke this way when he did things against the rules. I asked my sister if she thought my approach to discipline was acceptable. This was so mildly abusive compared to how our mother had treated us that neither of us could see that it was shaming!

Less obvious examples are calling sex nasty or dirty, or telling children not to touch their genitals or anus. Even frowning in discomfort communicates that the observed behavior is shame-worthy.

Judgments based on race, religion, gender, occupation, education, income, life style, sexual orientation, disability, intelligence, mental illness, and many other groupings are examples of groups of people shaming other groups of people.

Because I was studying shaming during the days I spent with my extended family I was tuned into the examples. Everyone shamed the children, and all the adults shamed each other. And the children shamed the adults. Then the children were told in angry voices not to talk that way. The children shamed and controlled each other in child versions of what the adults did.

This way of relating is seamlessly integrated into our society. A few years ago I would have felt discomfort, but not understood why. I have learned to recognize the small put-downs, and in particular, humorously delivered shame.

This family is normal, friendly and sociable. They welcome their friends openly and create warm social events. The parents are truly dedicated, wanting to do the best they can. Not only are they normal, they are exceptional. Yet they continually operate on acculturated shame, passing it along.

Shaming is set up by evaluating performance, even when the response to the behavior is positive. The child who reads more books than anyone in his class, and studies things he is interested in, is praised for being the best. Along with shaming, he is set up to think that his value is associated with what he does. Any time he fails to be the best, or even very good, he feels devastated. He feels shame.

The father of the one year old told him no, stop crying, stop reaching for the potatoes on the table. He gently slapped the boy's hand. This child is being taught that his normal, age-appropriate emotions and curiosity are bad. This translates directly to believing that he is bad because of course at that age his emotions are who he is. Our emotions are who we are. He is being conditioned to stop using the emotions of grief, which are necessary to move from era to era of life. He is trained to be not curious. It is not allowed to be part of his identity.

If we are shame-based our identity includes the belief that we are defective or bad.

This father is working hard to control his son and turn him into a child that is easy to be around. This could be lauded. However, the father is so out of touch with his son's appropriate emotions that he cannot know that what he is doing is harmful. It is clear that the father loves his son. He feels affection for him. He is responsible, making sure he isn't harmed, eats on time, gets his nap. He is doing all he is capable of based on the influence of the culture and his own childhood.

I watched another little boy excitedly tell his mother that he found a penny on the ground. She said in a shaming, aren't-you-stupid tone, "So you found a penny on the ground." If I told her she was shaming him, she might respond with how he finds so much on the ground and expects her to be excited about it when she has real problems to think about. She communicated to her son that he is stupid or wrong to be excited about finding a penny, when in fact, it is totally natural and human for a boy of his age to be excited.

The penny example of shame seems so small and subtle that most people would believe it couldn't possibly be harmful. Yet this is the kind of treatment that clients remember when working on depression or anxiety. One man said, "My mother always acted like I was just too stupid for words. Even when I got accepted to college, she said I should have been accepted to a better one. She didn't come to my graduation. So now I don't tell her how successful I am and how much money I make because I know she will somehow put it down."

Chapter 2: Ordinary, Everyday Shaming

Shaming is going on all around us all the time, and because it is "normal," is difficult to observe. I point out shaming to clients, friends, and occasionally strangers, and they shake their heads, looking puzzled. I can hear the voice in their heads saying, "What are you talking about?" A year or so later clients, who can now observe shaming, smile when a new group member has the same reaction.

During talks I gave, I got to see how difficult it is for people to recognize everyday shaming when I offered examples from my own life. As I presented information to my audience, I smiled and shook my head, tacitly putting the other person down.

I explained that I enjoyed telling this story in shaming tones, as it was an example of a time during which I had still felt like shaming. Then I presented the same experience in factual tones.

Audiences do not perceive that I am shaming, even when I say I am and then present the non-shaming alternative. Complaining about incomprehensible behavior is so accepted as normal and appropriate that rarely do members of audiences know that I was shaming. Healing starts with being able to perceive what ordinary shaming looks like. Each of us needs to know that when we feel defensive, or are uncomfortable with the tone directed at us, we may very well be the object of shaming. Watching movies, TV, and ads in a group is a way to study this. Stopping the show every three minutes to check for the presence of shaming will gradually reveal the ordinary variety.

In this culture, loaded with defensiveness and fear of feeling wronged or seen as a bad person, we are just as likely to get a bad reaction to boundary-setting as we are to shaming. Actually, shaming can usually be better tolerated because we are prepared for it! We can respond with our well-rehearsed defensive style, angrily attack back, and refuse to hear the boundary.

Learning to See Acculturated Shaming

Here are some statements I overheard in restaurants and malls. I will re-state them with stronger words with the same message, and finally, re-state them without shaming.

Frustrated Mother

A woman came in the swinging door of a health food store with two small children. One child opened the door which bumped my cart, and the second rolled the mat up as she scuffed her feet over it. The mother looked at me apologetically and told the children with annoyance that they were accidents waiting to happen.

Perhaps others would see this as critical, too, but still, it is also seen as entirely appropriate parenting. It is correct to complain about children. I thought so when I was the parent of a young child.

If would be easier to see if she said, "Get back, you idiot. And you, watch where you put your stupid feet! Whoever gave you the right to live in this world?"

What if she didn't shame? She might have reached out and grabbed the hand of each child, holding them outside the door until she saw that it was clear. She wouldn't have held them responsible for perceiving something they are too young to see. She knew that when they were two, they needed to have a hand held or be in a stroller. She doesn't understand what kind of restraint they need when they are a little older. She blames them for this.

Frustrating Teen:

The teenager came into the restaurant with her family, and as they walked to their table, she said, "I want to call Josh." Sounds innocent enough, but her tone communicated, "Why do I have to be here with you freaks, anyway, I so don't want to be here. You never let me do what I want." Can you imagine the tone?

If she were to have a boundary she might have told her parents that she was going to the parking lot to call Josh, and here's what to order, tell me when it's here. If the parents wanted a nice family dinner, they won't get to have her included. But she wouldn't have joined them anyway, so why not allow the boundary?

Angry Couple

I watched a couple through the window to the patio at Starbucks. They weren't speaking, but shame was flowing. The woman flipped her foot up and down and had a slight frown. If she had been by herself I would have wondered what was wrong. Since she was sitting opposite a man who was leaning forward with his head down, I didn't have to wonder. She was finding fault with him, and he felt like he deserved it. Their bodies said it all.

If she were to speak, she might have said, "Whatever possessed me to be married to you? I just can't believe that you have done this, and then hidden it from me. What were you thinking?" I didn't have to know what he did. It isn't the issue.

He has nothing to say. He is bad. He can't even defend himself by shaming back, by being defensive, by explaining it away. He has given up.

If she had been speaking clearly I would have expected something like, "I'm upset about what you did. I'm also upset that you felt the need to hide it from me. I have a lot of thinking to do about this, I'm not sure what it means about trusting you." She would have looked right at him and spoken with no criticism, just concern and feelings.

He would respond with shame, as apparently he did something hurtful. But then grief would follow because he knows that he has done something that can't be undone. He has to regain her trust, however, before that can happen.

Delivery of Information

I counsel husbands to set boundaries around how much blame and hurt they will receive, instead asking for straightforward information and expression of emotions.

I address the difference between the communication of shame and the delivery of information. The very same words can convey valuable information to a spouse, or communicate that the spouse is wrong and stupid and had better change.

It is understood that children who are physically, emotionally and sexually abused will internalize shame. They will have psychological, social and medical outcomes. Psychotherapy for trauma has evolved in order to assist in grieving away the experiences, which includes removing the shame that is woven into their very identity.

Now we can heal from the
ordinary, everyday shaming
going on all around us.

We need to address acculturated shame. Healing begins with recognizing the mild, everyday forms. Then, we can stop this shame from coming in. Then we can learn to stop shaming others.

It is difficult to describe acculturated shaming because it is accepted as normal. It takes time for couples to see how they shame each other.

Voice Tone

Tone communicates as much as words. Ask any dog. A couple sits in my office. The wife says that she doesn't know if she wants to continue the marriage because he flirts with other women, and calls her names. Name-calling is obviously shaming, as is telling people they are defective. Both the husband and the wife could see this.

However, neither recognized that she was shaming him with her tone. She had a mildly hurt, how-could-you-do-this-to-me tone. He reacted defensively. When I pointed out her tone, she argued with me. I asked her to notice how her voice was coming from her throat, not from down in her chest. When she could speak from a deeply felt, empowered place, she was able to give him the same information but without shaming him. He was still defensive, but less so.

When feeling like a victim (different from being truly victimized), people will present their experience in a shaming manner whether the subject is government, the banking system, other drivers, spouses, family members, children, politicians, or anyone else who is believed to be doing something wrong. A non-shaming response is forward-moving, information-stating, with the voice coming from the chest. There is no head-shaking. No implication of, "How could they do this!"

Gossip is a form of joining with others to shame those who are bad, stupid, thoughtless, too wealthy, too fat, too anything not approved of.

When an investment partner and I had to foreclose on a property, we expressed victimized shock at the owner's ongoing lies and manipulations accompanied by tears and regret. When I pulled us out of this reaction, we were able to see that the owner was willing to violate his integrity to try to retain the property, and we could comfortably stand our ground. Not feeling shame for causing his distress, we didn't have to shame him for his manipulations. When we stopped shaming him, we stopped wasting time and energy. We could clearly see what was called for.

When a client laughs too loudly, or says something "inappropriate," his wife gives him a look, or makes a sound, or says his name. She shames him in a culturally accepted manner. Others in the room may join her with chuckles and smiles and nods. Whenever people are out of touch and do odd things, others are allowed to shame them. Then everyone lives in fear of doing odd things, and being shamed for it!

I sat at dinner while my friend shamed her husband with no words. She didn't even look at him shamingly. Her energy was hardened, and she appeared separate from him even though they sat a few inches apart. She didn't know her anger was shaming him. He responded defensively. He didn't know that her reaction to what he had done was not healthy. I described the scene, and they both understood, although it took time for them to change their behavior.

A client who applied for a line of credit told me how he "won" when his bank had required proof of income at the last minute. He got an explanation, but when it didn't suit him, he cancelled his application. His tone said he had gotten one over on them. He relieved his own shame by shaming them, even though he hadn't gotten his credit line.

When I pointed this out, another man in the group said, "Showed them!" He wanted to triangulate with me against the other client, but with humor so the man wouldn't be offended. He was inviting him into a classic maneuver to relieve his shame. Laugh together.

Women's acculturated shaming is more difficult to see than men's because women are the good gender. We are entitled to shame men for being boorish pigs, too interested in themselves, not adequately meeting our needs.

Men's shame is easier to see because men are the bad gender. When they shame others it is seen as bad. They are more overt when they tell women what is wrong with them. Of course they pay for it because they receive invisible shaming in return. Even when women name-call, it is not perceived to be as harmful because men are seen as deserving it! Both genders shame equally, and the shaming of both genders is equally harmful.

Watch. Listen. Notice. Feel. Sigh. Breathe. Talk.

My job is getting shaming spouses to change how they speak to each other. I worked with one woman on how she said, "I don't like that," to her husband. When she held herself back, she looked at him sideways, her soft voice communicating that he was really bad for doing something she didn't like. When she was able to fully claim her dislike for what he did, and say it straight out, looking him in the eyes, she was merely expressing what she felt, what was going on inside of her. There was no shaming. Just facts.

We don't see acculturated shaming going on all the time. When Cathy Lee Gifford made fun of Larry King on national television for everything he said, including not remembering what was in his autobiography, it was seen by her and the audience as funny. You are supposed to be a good sport when shame is delivered as humor. He would be seen as a wimp for telling her to stop.

Critical, condescending humor is considered entertaining, bonding and witty.
It is shaming.

When Larry King was on The View, Barbara Walters shamingly peppered him with the question, why didn't he search for his son, Larry King, Jr., until the son was 30? She did this to invite the audience to triangulate with her against Larry. Then she pulled out of it by complimenting him for putting this information in his autobiography. She abused him, and then rescued him from her abuse. This is typical of her interview style. Why did this make her popular? Do women enjoy watching another woman shame men? Is it seeing someone shame celebrities and powerful people? Or is it enjoying the shaming of anyone?

Why is a yawning cat the cutest thing ever but people are supposed to hide their own yawning?

Notice how many TV ads shame one of the actors, and indirectly, shame you for not buying something.

Embarrassment

Many people say they don't feel shame, they're just embarrassed, or uncomfortable. Shame is on a continuum from mild discomfort to intensely hideous emotional pain. Embarrassment and discomfort are at the milder end and are less likely to be identified as shame.

As we educate ourselves about this everyday shame, we can see how often we and others receive and deliver it. A sure signal is any need to claim that we aren't shame-worthy or shame-deserving. Studying defensiveness might be easier than identifying shame, as it is not so hidden. Notice when you hold back, or have a slight frown as you try to prove that what you believe is true. More intense defensiveness, of course, includes counter-attack, loudness, refusing to listen, classic circular arguments where both people defend, and physical violence.

Study the ordinary, everyday defensiveness. This is where the education can come from. When you say, "How can you think that?" or "Why did you say that?" notice if there is protest in your voice. Notice if it is a true, straight-out question.

Rudeness

Countless clients have looked at me seriously as they ask, "But isn't that rude?" Or they say, "I don't want to be rude."

Rude is a shaming word. It can be replaced by a description of the behavior, and a boundary. "When you keep pushing me along, it makes me uncomfortable and please stop." "You keep interrupting me and I'd like to finish what I was saying." The behaviors are addressed with boundaries. Calling them rude merely shames the person and does not create a boundary.

"Respect" is another common shaming word. While we want to be respected, telling someone that they don't respect you doesn't communicate what you need. What is the behavior that doesn't feel respectful? Instead of "you are so disrespectful when you come late all the time," you could say, "I'm not willing to wait for you when you are late." This isn't shaming. It's having a boundary.

Classic Ordinary Shaming Sentences

How often do you hear words such as thoughtless, selfish, rude, inconsiderate, unkind, stupid, crazy, negative, dumb, liar, and cheater? Let us hope not often directed at you! These words are integrated into our language, and only seen as shaming if they are spoken in a harsh, shaming tone. "You are such an idiot!!" We all agree that's shaming. But what if someone says in a normal tone, "Honey, that wasn't very thoughtful, was it? What do you think you might have done instead?" This is more difficult to see as shaming. Or, with humor, "Oh my god, I was so stupid, what was I thinking?" Or a friend's embarrassment at not having vacuumed, which implies that you are criticizing her for it. She reacts as if you have shamed her, when the shame is internally generated. But you have to say, No problem, I don't mind, in order to relieve her shame, and to make it clear that you aren't shaming her.

Suspiciousness

Suspicious tones are shaming. Non-shaming would be asking directly for information and receive an answer. The woman at the customer service counter, who was required to leave her package before entering the store, said, "What are you going to do with it?" This question could have been a clear request for information, but her suspicious tone said the customer service woman was sure to lose it or steal it. She was expressing shaming anger that had nothing to do with the woman behind the counter.

Impatience

Impatience is shaming. It implies that the person is doing something wrong, or too slowly. Being impatient when children "dawdle," a shaming word, tells them that they are misbehaving. In truth, young children have no internal programming to alert them that timing is important, and only cooperate because it is required. If this is understood, then the parent could set up a reward system so the child gets something for doing something that to him has no meaning. This reward brings some external meaning. A payment. Shaming a child for not being obedient doesn't support cooperation.

Impatience is a shaming alternative to setting boundaries. One wife complained about playing the waiting game as she criticized her husband to other wives. He never left on time for social events or church services.

It wasn't within her perception of herself and her marriage to take her own car and leave on time. If she understands that she is shaming her husband, and engendering his unexpressed anger, she can practice developing new boundaries and give up shaming.

Defensiveness

Defensiveness is a sign that someone is feeling shame and wants to turn it on the other person. I keep repeating this because defensiveness is such a vital emotion to understand when learning about shame. We all feel shame. We all feel defensive. Everyone around us feels shame. Everyone around us will be defensive.

When a boss tells an employee that the performance isn't up to standard, the employee may defensively argue, explain why he didn't do well, or claim that he is doing fine. His tone indicates whether this is information or is accompanied by a defensive attitude, a shame-based desire to make the evaluation untrue. The boss may have spoken with a put-down shaming tone, or he may have just given information. Either way, most people will feel shame for not being viewed as adequate. The person who can't argue with the boss might tell friends or a mate how unfair or wrong the boss was. Or he might believe the boss is right, and feel full-out shame.

Defensiveness goes on all around us. A customer asks why the store no longer carries a brand of cat food, and the manager makes a case for why that brand shouldn't be carried. When the nutritionist argued with me about sugar, she shook her head as if I were attacking her personally for wanting me to eat ice cream. When I called my phone company's advertising section to ask why I was billed for a service I had cancelled, the woman's tone defensively implied that I was not very bright because I couldn't take her word for the charges.

Anytime someone thinks they haven't done something in accordance with social values and rules and requirements, such as getting poor grades or making mistakes or providing poor parenting or thousands of other possibilities, defensiveness is a likely reaction to ward off shame.

Accepting Shaming

Shaming is so integrated into the culture that people find it easier to be shamed than told a painful truth. A friend showed up for our meeting really late. What if I shamed him by saying, "God, that was really thoughtless, how could you think I should just wait around for you?" He could have said he was sorry, or defensively explained that it was on account of traffic and his phone died, or told me I'm too demanding. But if I looked him in the eye and spoke in a straightforward, honest voice with no shaming to tell him that I don't like what he did, he has no culturally approved way to cope with it. He would feel toxic shame.

Criticism

Criticizing table manners or driving, telling someone in a whiny tone that they're doing something wrong, treating others as if they don't have the same rights, are common forms of shaming.

Constructive criticism is supposed to be the non-shaming variety. But constructive criticism can be delivered with a shaming tone, too. Bosses need to convey information when a job isn't done correctly, or could be done more efficiently. This is constructive and appropriate. However, if the tone implies that the employee should have already known, or the boss is superior, or if the words are impatiently delivered, then shame is interwoven with the information.

Because criticism is usually perceived as shaming, it is hard for most people to deliver it. Working with newer clients, I remain aware of how they may receive the useful information I offer. Even knowing I'm not shaming, they can very well feel shame anyway. Any feedback about what we are doing that isn't good for us or for others, or that is far from perfect, is considered shameful in this culture. Over time my clients come to appreciate that my information is useful, and are able to receive it without feeling shamed.

A friend studied how she shames her husband. She mentioned his wrinkled pants and the choice of shirt when he met with wealthy clients, and how he then freezes up. His shame prevents him from having boundaries. He can't say, "These wrinkles are acceptable to me. These clients are more interested in what I can do for them than in my shirt. Don't criticize me."

A client gave me two recent examples from his life that he became able to see as shaming, when before he would have questioned himself. At a renowned zoo he showed his tickets, wondering aloud if he needed a different kind. The woman shoved them back at him, saying "Can't you read?" with disgust. He didn't know that he had a ticket that qualified for any exhibit.

The second instance took place at his bank, where he asked why a deposit hadn't been recorded on his line of credit. The banker explained that he had put it in the wrong account. She handed the paperwork back to him, and said, "Mr. D., you should have known!"

Now that he knows this is shaming, he can let it slide on by. When he didn't have that objectivity, he felt shame!

*Every one of us has to learn to
see shaming that is
woven into the culture, and
refuse to take it in.*

This client carried a great load of shame beginning with having been unloved as a child, shamed throughout childhood because of being odd and not fitting in, and then from alcoholism and extra-marital affairs. In spite of all of this he is learning to see shaming, to refuse to take it in even from his wife, and gradually stop his angry response to it. Observing all around us, including family members, allows the shaming to become clear, to be seen as outside the self, and to understand that it can be healed.

Competition

Competing with the implication that winning makes one better than the losers shames everyone. Team sports, even at the elementary school level, provoke shaming from parents, classmates and spectators. Even the winners feel shame because they know they could be and have been the losers. Needing to win in order to avoid bad feeling leaves one vulnerable the next time. People who have been very successful in their careers can feel devastated when unable to continue, such as after retirement. They can no longer win.

Everyday Shaming

You know how it feels when someone pushes past you in a store, implying that you were in the way? Or a driver honks because you were in the wrong lane or cut him off? These are examples of everyday shaming.

The boss frowns at you when you are three minutes late to a meeting. A co-worker thinks she is doing more than her share and shuns you in the lounge. An employee treats you like the father who abused her, she's afraid of you and walked on egg shells. The woman standing in the bank line glares at everyone.

A common shaming from parents and others is to ask, "What makes you think you could do that?" When I was writing my fifth book in a park, a man asked me what I was doing, then proceeded to tell me that it's not easy to write a book and get it published, what made me think I could? I thought he was strange, but didn't realize that he enjoyed shaming others and I was handy. He failed because I told him I had a major publisher, and had already published books. I felt victorious as I put him in his place. Now I see that he was medicating his shame by perceiving me as a stupid woman who thought she could do something done by few. I didn't win anything. I merely prevented him from diminishing his feelings of shame. He had to find another alternative.

Even harsher shaming is the question, "What makes you think you deserve that?" When a friend was in high school, her troop won a competition that entitled it to a free trip to Japan. She was excited until her mother asked her that question. Her mother's own miserable life had made her jealous of her daughter, so she took the edge off her pleasure by making her clean tile grout with a toothbrush in order to earn the necessary pocket money. While this is seen as mean by the culture, it is harder to see that the daughter would experience this as communication of her lack of worth. When a mother doesn't feel loving and delighted for her daughter's success, the girl can take it to mean there is something wrong with her, even while she and her friends say it's the mother who is bad.

Managing the Emotions of Others

When people are cautious and reluctant and hesitant, they might elicit feelings of shame in others. When you are on the receiving end you are being seen as someone who people need to be reluctant and hesitant around.

Acting hesitant communicates that the other person is dangerous, and has to be managed even though it is an internal experience. When my co-healer was reluctant and apologetic, I got annoyed. As we processed, I saw that I have taken on shame when people acted as if I could hurt them, and as if they had to be careful around me. Then I realized that it was just her fear from having to manage both of her parents to avoid emotional abuse. She had projected it onto me and everyone around her. I had to understand this in order to not take on shame.

If you think back on conversations in which the other person was hesitant to tell you what they were going to do, or about an experience they had, what did you feel? You might not have felt shame because your methods to avoid it were engaged. My own reaction was anger. I was objecting to the implication that I was dangerous and the other person had to handle me to keep me from reacting in bad ways. My mother had seen me this way in childhood and that experience had been activated.

When people are afraid of you they are shaming you. That is unless you are someone to be afraid of.

An example of invisible shaming occurred when a friend talked with an acquaintance. The acquaintance asked him questions about still being at the same job, the tone implying that he had not bettered himself. The friend responded defensively, a signal that he was being shamed, and felt shame. In order to not feel shame, he first needed to see that he was being shamed.

Do you manage the emotions of others? Do you hold back information so the other person doesn't become angry, shame-filled, abandoning, or shaming? What do you do to manage those potential reactions? Do you smile, or use an affectionate tone of voice, or change the subject to something neutral?

Notice why you want to do that. Perhaps it's to avoid having the other person feel the shame you expect if you were to be right out there with your comments.

Most people apologize for actions that don't warrant apologizing. Common examples are: not remembering or misunderstanding something someone said, forgetting someone's name, not hearing correctly, not knowing the answer to a question, walking too fast or too slowly, wearing the wrong clothes, choosing the wrong movie or restaurant or gift. What about running into someone's basket in the store, walking into someone when you couldn't see them coming, and on and on.

Forgetting someone's name, or what they said, is seen as not valuing that person when in truth, it's just not remembering. Many of us have poor memories. Not only can I not remember names, I can't remember faces. A co-investor and I met very many people over the course of our business. He remembered them all, I remembered few. He soon learned to tell me who the person was, and then I explained to them that I have poor visual memory. I felt no shame about this, and in time he lost his own at pointing this out in front of the person. He helped me avoid having the person feel slighted or making other interpretations of my not responding to them. He helped me present the truth. He learned that he could help both of us, and feel good, not shameful.

If you know it is your memory, and that you are not slighting someone, there is no reason for shame, healthy or toxic. Instead of saying I'm sorry, I explain that it's my memory. This is the truth.

Isn't it odd that we feel shame when not understanding what someone said? If neither the speaker nor listener has shame, then it quickly becomes obvious that communication hasn't occurred. Facial expressions register confusion. Then one person can say, I don't think I heard you correctly, or the other says, I don't think you heard me correctly. Then they go back and do it again. Shame comes when the listener thinks he must hear correctly. Then the speaker feels as if she has to make sure the listener doesn't feel shame. Or, she shames him for not understanding.

Then there are the really ordinary areas of shame agreed upon by all. You are shame-worthy if you have underarm sweat (unless you just worked out), stains, wrinkles or cat hair on clothing, smelly gas, skin wrinkles, fat, inadequate social skills, lack of sex appeal, if you are drunk, going to work late, breaking engagements at the last minute. Perhaps healthy shame is appropriate for some of these, but toxic shame for any will prevent change. Contrary to popular belief, shame doesn't help us change from the inside out. I overheard a young man swimming laps get out of the pool and berate himself for doing poorly. He sounded like his own shaming coach.

Shaming Others

The culture agrees that we should feel shame for shaming, and shame for just having shame.

When discovering the shaming going on all around us all the time, many people start looking at how they shame others. Parents can find this difficult because it means looking at how they shame their children. I really want to acknowledge that everyone shames, including me. You shame others. If you are a parent of course you have shamed your children.

The first step in healing shame is accepting that every single one of us has shamed others. We have all been mean. We have all harmed. There is no way around this.

If we feel compelled to prove that we haven't harmed anyone, our shame will multiply. I was relieved to realize that I along with everyone else has harmed. It is unavoidable because of the culture we all grew up in. Shaming was modeled. We were shamed if we didn't shame in the manner our parents did. Then we are shamed for not shaming in the manner our peers did. We were shamed for not joining others in shaming political parties, the boss, anything in the news.

Most people feel shame for just having shame. What an incredibly difficult conundrum this is! If you feel shame just for having shame, it makes it difficult to take a look at your shame! This is why working with a group of people who are all healing is helpful. You can look around the room at others who feel it, and know that they shouldn't have to. This knowing then has a chance of being reflected back onto you.

When I tell people that very little apology is appropriate, they frequently argue with me. They say they don't want to be rude. When I described mutual crashing of grocery carts, and laughing together over it with no apology, several audience members believed that apology was needed. A couple couldn't hear that I was talking about mutual crashing, not one person crashing into another. Yet, even then, I don't apologize. I say something like, Oh, I wasn't watching where I was going. Or, I didn't see you around that corner. Or, Oops! This feels appropriate when I haven't intended to hit someone.

The woman at the bank took my deposit with an annoyed expression. Even if she didn't know she was shaming, she was. When done, she smiled and said have a nice day, but she was acting. I know this had nothing to do with me. I wasn't affected because I could see it. At the emergency vet's I was the same person, but received three different reactions. The couple with the sick dog wanted to engage me; the receptionist, without saying a word, acted as though I were a bother and should sit down and shut up; and the vet was friendly, business-like and efficient.

When someone is irritated with you they are holding you responsible for something, which shames you.

If you are unable to set boundaries, you are likely to shame others for the very things that you could yourself claim.

A client presented a list of the ways in which his wife and daughter treated him like a convenience instead of a person. He felt compelled to let them have their way, and so with an impatient tone and body language, he shamed them. As he learned how each situation could have been handled differently, he saw how his family members would have responded favorably. With small and easy-to-set-boundaries, his irritation wouldn't have grown, and he wouldn't have felt shamed.

We learned that he was projecting his parents onto his wife and daughter, as his only value was what he did for them. In the present, all he had to do was not carry all the bags. Hand them out. Not take a backseat. Instead of pouting, he could have engaged both wife and daughter. When he was unable to perceive his right to boundaries regarding his role in the family, he couldn't do anything but pout and shame them.

Shaming is sometimes called anger. It isn't anger. It's shaming. Healthy, discharging anger doesn't shame!

I explain to couples that when they hold anger back, it is likely to come out as shaming. Converting anger into feeling hurt is a way that women typically avoid anger. What isn't seen is that telling someone that they hurt you is a form of shaming. And it doesn't offer a recourse for healing. If someone tells you that she is really angry about what you did, and directs it right at you, she can discharge the anger and grieve it away. A process leading to a conclusion becomes possible. Shaming, on the other hand, won't lead anywhere.

Dr. Phil shames his TV guests, his tone asking how they could possibly think that was acceptable behavior. He invites the audience to triangulate with him against the guests.

Parents shame children with a critical tone even when their words are neutral. They do this with impatience and sighs. Exasperation. The sigh says, You are so bad, uncontrollable, that I just give up. This gives the power to the child because the parent is relinquishing it.

Sighs of displeasure shame. These sighs are so different from those expressing satisfaction and understanding and robust delight. These are hopeless, giving up. Shaming.

Self-shaming

Even after years of studying shaming and healing my own, I discovered that I have my own self-shaming! I apologize for my poor memory. Now with understanding, I stop myself and say, "Oh, I'm shaming myself. I'm going to say this again." I get to see what it is like to stop! It took focus on the very ordinary shame to stop acculturated self-criticism.

Chapter 3: Recognizing Shaming

Years ago I set out to learn to recognize when people were shaming me. It was a slow education as our culture accepts so much shaming as normal, natural and right. If we can't see when we are being shamed, we will take it in, adding one more piece to the layers. It's easier to refuse what we can see. So we need to see.

Since shaming is so woven into the culture, most of it is invisible. Subtle shaming remains fuzzy and out of focus until we have observed it long enough to see it. Only the more obvious comments are seen, such as: What's wrong with you? How could you do that to me? Shame on you! You're so stupid!

While a couple stood waiting for their drinks at Starbucks, the woman spoke to the man in a quiet, constrained voice as she explained why she wasn't going out with him that evening. The people he wanted to go out with were drinkers who became abusive as the evening went on, she explained. These words could have conveyed no shame, but her tightly held mouth, frown, and rigid body revealed her anger that he even suggested she should go. Her shaming indicated that he shouldn't go, either.

The man defended his friends, saying that they could leave if anyone seemed drunk. If they did he didn't want to stay either. He shamed her back with his tone which communicated that she was horrible for treating him as if he were thoughtless and inconsiderate.

The other customers didn't seem to notice. This interaction was entirely within the norm. One or two people might have curiously looked over. They wouldn't see the harm caused, they would see nothing more than a couple in conflict.

Shame healers are aware of much more. We hear the tone, and bring into focus the experience of the man being shamed. They would see that the woman couldn't have a boundary and not go with him. She couldn't express a preference that he not go. And he couldn't ask her to tell him what she wanted without seeing him as thoughtless, unkind and selfish.

Join me in fine-tuning a perception of shaming that is invisible to the acculturated eye.

Shame woven into normal conversation harms all levels of our identity. Our physical, emotional, mental, spiritual, social, behavioral and life-style facets are condemned all the time. Then the internalization of such shaming makes us believe that we are basically bad, and must follow certain rules to be seen as good.

Physical shaming includes shaming body functions. I overheard women in a locker room of a gym compared each other's bodies to see where each rates. All agree that being overweight is shame-worthy, along with flab, cellulite, and wrinkles.

Women diet, thinking self-esteem will arrive when they reach the right weight. But the internalized shame doesn't go away. She is still too short, too tall, not the right shape, her skin imperfect, her head too small, mouth too big, shoulders too broad. And breasts! It's now easy to buy "right" looking ones.

Mental shaming is passed onto every child going to school. All are compared against a standard instead of helped to develop individual interests and gifts. Being below average in intelligence is seen as something to laugh at or condemn. Yet below average means half of all people. Smart people are shamed, too. Those who consider themselves not smart enough take pleasure when a smart person gets something wrong.

Emotional shaming is called abusive when it's extreme. However, the ordinary versions are woven into the culture. They include treating others as if they are inferior, can't love well, don't pay enough attention to their partner, don't interact appropriately with co-workers. These assessments make a person feel badly. It is a major cause of lack of self-esteem.

Spiritual shaming comes from living in a culture that believes that rule-following makes you good, where religion becomes rules to follow. Internalized shame has prevented almost everyone from knowing how we are designed to interact and our real purpose.

Social shaming makes social drinking popular. As alcohol makes fear and shame slide away, it becomes possible to have a better time in social situations. People who have difficulty conversing or whose shame prevents them from relating with interest are put down even by the facial expressions of others.

Behavioral shaming can be seen in sports where a player is valued for performing well and put down for not. Children are shamed for not behaving, for not being ready on time, for not staying in bed, for fighting with siblings, for lack of obedience, and much more.

Lifestyle shaming is reflected in the phrase, "Keeping up with the Joneses." People feel shame, and are shamed, for living on little, and for being too wealthy. Rich people are envied as well as shamed for having too much. No one can create a lifestyle that won't be shamed by someone.

You can question if you are being shamed by looking at how you feel. This isn't foolproof because people often feel shame when information is delivered shame-free. It's a good place to start, though. For example, while one server in a restaurant may make you feel good as you exchange information about food, another may be indifferent, and you have no reaction. When the third asks for your order, you may have an odd sensation of being put down, or that it's too much work to wait on you, or a bother. Something is wrong with you. If you check this person out, you may get other clues.

In a gourmet Santa Monica restaurant, my friend and I noticed that the woman seating us was rushed, pushing our menus at us before we could even sit down. We sort of fell into our chairs with huge menus in our hands and purses on our arms. The server came over and stood with feet wide apart, head slightly back, staring down at us. I had looked at the menu and seen ingredients I didn't care for, and asked if the sauces could be switched. He frowned, shaking his head slightly, as he explained that the chef had come up with excellent combinations of flavors that weren't to be changed. He acted as though we weren't quite smart enough to understand.

My friend had eaten there many times, and found this treatment very different from what she had come to expect. I guessed that either we weren't dressed properly or the server was afraid of losing his job. She later learned that the chef was worried about the restaurant closing because the economy had reduced his business. The staff was clearly affected by fear, and weren't present to those of us there for dinner.

Our need to be treated graciously in an expensive restaurant while served a chef's original gourmet dishes wasn't met. If we had not seen what was going on, and had taken it personally, we would have consumed a little more shame. The classic response to this treatment is to turn it back on the staff - complain how poorly they treat their customers, they should be fired, "how does this place stay in business?"

Counter-shaming reduces the feeling of shame.

We needed information in order to not do what babies do and assume it was something we had done, or merely who we were. The staff's behavior implied that we weren't worth their attention. This was clearly not true. They needed us. They needed our business and our money. Their fear and impending shame from losing a job and a business didn't allow them to see us - to see our needs.

They reacted in their habitual ways of avoiding shame and fear. The hostess was so out of touch with herself that she couldn't perceive how to treat us. We were no more than furniture. Mothers of babies can react the same way for the same reason.

I won't go to the restaurant again. I missed out on the experiences of eating an amazing, unique meal, and the friendly communing over this experience that enhances the pleasure of new flavors.

My friend and I weren't harmed by the shaming because we could see it, know that it was caused by things we didn't understand, and that it truly wasn't about what we wore or the questions we asked.

Some Mexican-Americans in Southern California carry shame as a result of decades of shaming directed toward them. I drove by two men who seemed to assume that I was racist and shaming them. When I lived here 35 years ago, these people carried such obvious shame I assumed it was characteristic of Mexicans. When I visited Mexico, I saw an entirely different people! Then I knew that those in Southern California were suffering from racism. I was deeply pleased when returning here to see that this is no longer true. The Mexican-American population, now with many who grew up here while maintaining their language and cultural heritage, carries comparatively little shame. Those men are now the exception.

When a young man with tattoos, piercings and attitude approached a bank teller, she communicated disgust and contempt with her expression. He was uncomfortable as he was new to banking. He didn't know he needed his card or a deposit slip. He received her silent shaming, added onto the internalized layers. While he may very well have been a gang member who does bad things, I felt sorry for him. I wanted her and everyone to welcome him into the world with genuine caring.

Self-Shaming

After receiving shaming for decades, we fall into a natural shaming of ourselves. If we feel compelled to believe that the culture and parents and others are correct, then it is only natural to turn on ourselves as well. "How could I have done that?" "What was I thinking?" "I'm so stupid." "Can you ever forgive me?"

Self-shaming is seen as low self-esteem. It prevents developing one's gifts, completing needed education or training, or other approaches to living fully. Self-doubt, self-criticism, immobility, apathy, and depression are only some of the ways self-shaming inhibits living a full life.

As I studied every sign of shame while writing about it, I noticed one of my own, very ordinary examples. My wood floors quickly go from lovely to layered with cat hair and dirt, the price of having little creatures living with me. If a close friend drops in I ignore the floor, but if someone I don't know well is coming, especially if they haven't been in my house before, I feel compelled to sweep it. If I don't, then I have to acknowledge to my guests that the floor is a mess.

I saw that I was trying to say that really, I have clean floors, they just aren't at the moment. I'm a cleaner person than this. Please believe me!

Once I saw this, I deliberately observed myself when a friend came over. I deliberately didn't sweep, and just felt the shame. As it flowed out of me, I laughed at the absurdity of evaluating myself based on how much cat hair was on the floor!

The Victim Triangle

This triangle of victim, rescuer and abuser relating has been called a variety of names. I think that it might best be called the Shame Triangle. All three positions are designed to inhibit the experience of shame. If you can recognize when people are playing parts in this configuration instead of living fully, recognizing shaming will be easier.

Addiction recovery circles understand this determinant of much social relating. Assuming the roles of victim, abuser, and rescuer is not about genuine victimization, or really needed caretaking. Anytime people operate in the triangle, they aren't living in the present. Emotions are made up. Each of the three points are entered in order to avoid internalized shame. All of us can operate in any of the points, but tend to prefer one. Rescue seems the nicest, kindest, but it is just as false and shame-based as the other two.

Victim Position in the Triangle

Victim behavior is very common in our culture. Whenever a person complains about something unfair, hurtful, mean, critical, or incompetent, he or she is shifting into a victim mentality. The healthy approach is discussing issues, problems, and conflicts with the attitude of what can be done to solve them. Anything else is merely a way to pass time. Criticizing politicians, bosses, employees, family members, etc., in a manner that doesn't impart information or seek a solution is engaging in victim mentality.

Victim shaming is a common American pastime, often conducted over drinks or coffee or an evening with friends. Now that I don't join such exchanges, I have become unpopular with those who value them. If I say nothing, others' shame is often triggered. They feel judged by me, even while I am just observing.

To take the victim position is by definition, shaming. If you feel like my victim, then you must see me as harming you. Abusing you! If you think I should have called you two days ago, or I should have acknowledged your birthday, or remembered that you are spending the day with another friend, or in any way find fault from a victim stance, you will be shaming me. A straightforward approach might include healthy anger, tears and other emotions. A healthy response will hold me accountable for actual things I have done, but it won't shame me for them.

Conversations of victims bonding against perceived abusers create a sense of bonding together. Us against them. What's wrong with them, why do that do that, don't they know anything, why don't they know? The speakers are righteous, knowing they are right and the people they criticize are wrong. They are relieved from shame. They truly feel good.

Being the object of this kind of criticism is painful. Everyone who hasn't healed their internalized shame, which is almost everyone, will find it painful to overhear this kind of conversation about yourself. It can create unforgivable rifts, cause people to not speak to each other for years, and have arguments with back and forth shame-throwing.

It is commonly thought that people higher on the value scale receive less shame than those lower down. Poor people feel automatically shamed by the wealthy. The uneducated feel judged by the educated. Employees feel one down to bosses. However, those higher on the scale receive just as much shaming when those lower down adopt the victim stance. When they feel abused by those above them merely because they are above them they are shaming those at the higher level.

A woman working for a former publisher of mine set up a workshop for me to lead, and when it was over, told me that I didn't give her any appreciation. She was shaming me for having done something wrong. If she wanted to know if I thought she did a good job, she could have said, "Anne, are you satisfied with how I handled this?" Then we would have been equals. I could have said, "Yes, you had everything organized and it went smoothly. I hope we get to do this together again."

Victim shaming is perhaps the most difficult to recognize because victims feel as if they are on the receiving end of harm. How could they be the harming one? When their shaming is named, they might again feel victimized, and deliver more shaming.

There are many kinds of victim stances. These include hostile victim, angry victim, powerless victim, needy victim, shaming victim, mean victim, passive-aggressive victim.

As Lisa's victimization by her step father graduated into a victim identity, she directed critical-victim and hurt-victim and violated-victim onto the men she married. They were both abusive, and so from a cultural perspective, shaming them made sense. However, when understanding shaming, it can be seen that it engendered their rage and abuse. She couldn't figure out what she needed and present that in a straightforward, honest way. The abusive victim presentation, however, left her feeling powerless, while the man felt hideously shamed. A deadly combination.

Lisa's emotional healing included exploring the real powerlessness in childhood, and the shame that came with it. As she grieved it away, she could see how she had tortured her husbands, shaming them, and then suffering their methods of handling it. She could see that understanding her need for boundaries was essential in order to not abuse others. She had to heal her own shame to achieve that.

Fearing Others Shames Them

If people are afraid of you, they are shaming you by seeing you as potentially harmful. They may not know they are shaming, and can't stop if they did. We need to see when people are afraid of us so we don't take it on. Of the four office managers I have had, three saw themselves as my personal equal, did their work, and got paid. We worked well together. The fourth was afraid of me, afraid that I was going to fire her, and was uncomfortable around me no matter how hard I tried to rescue her. I finally gave up, and scheduled so that we weren't in the office at the same time. That boundary felt better because I wasn't comfortable being viewed as harmful, or potentially harmful.

Triangulated Marriage

Wives commonly take the victim position in marriage, blaming the husband for everything he does wrong. The culture supports this, and supports him in taking the shaming. She is the good gender, he is the bad. It also supports him in being passive-aggressive instead of setting boundaries by telling her that she isn't to shame him. As men and women become educated about shame, they have a better chance of forming good relationships. Once shaming is stopped, the opportunity to use healthy emotions to resolve conflicts improves.

Whenever people take a victim stance, they are shaming others.

Something to Try

Meet with friends or acquaintances you know are likely to discuss politics or religion or the economy or their health. Step back and listen. Notice how their voices change as they engage in a topic with victim-shaming. Do they become more lively? Do they smile? Do they frown with a how-can-they-do-this-to-me quality? Or do they take a how-could-they-be-so-stupid attitude? Do they shake their heads?

Try not joining in. Listen impassively. Does anyone react to you? Do they try to get you to join? How does it feel to not join? Do you feel a tug in order to avoid feeling on the outside? Or judged? If you maintain your listening stance, do they change how they address you? Do they stop triangulating? Do they go on, leaving you on the sidelines? Do they criticize you for being silent? Do they rescue you, perhaps with concern that you aren't feeling well? How do they try to make sense of your behavior?

A relative enjoys gossiping and putting others down. She describes their emotional and physical difficulties. She is addicted to substances that are destroying her health, and has a handicapped parking permit. I didn't join her in a helpless look at those "poor people" she described. For example, I told her that her daughter-in-law with obsessive compulsive disorder would be helped by intensive psychotherapy along with a certain anti-depressant. Even though this woman was speaking to an expert on mental illness, she brushed me aside, saying that the young woman was managing well, and didn't need help.

This woman energizes herself by shaming others, and therefore has no interest in learning how to help them. The intensity of her need to avoid her own shame prevents it. If I had felt obligated to control her into helping her daughter-in-law, I would have shamed her with my tone, and by the very belief that she needed to be controlled into being different. Instead I sat back and noticed what was going on. I accepted that there was nothing I could do. That brings freedom. I would recommend that anytime you find yourself having strong feelings about what someone else is doing, step back and observe. The desire to shame others to stop them from shaming may appear! The healing task is to just notice it.

Healing

If you gather your shame healers together to study shame, you can devise signals to alert each other to stop and observe. A touch on the arm can communicate. You may ask your friend to speak to the others so you can step back and observe. See if you can pull your attention to the study of shame, and away from your reactions to shaming.

When away from the shamers, catalog what went on. Look at how they were medicating their shame. Notice how they felt when you didn't join them. Observe what they did about it. See each example of shaming including toward the object of their conversation, toward you, toward each other. Notice if you wanted to shame anyone. Notice if your shame was triggered, and by what.

This education will automatically lead to change because you are removing cultural denial of culturally-approved shaming. As long as denial is in place, we can't see, and if we can't see we can't change.

Abuser Position in the Triangle

The very word, abuser, indicates that shame is on the way. This is one point in the triangle that is understandable to everyone. The person who yells or criticizes or hits is indicating that you are terrible and deserve such treatment. However, all points in the triangle shame all the others, and so actually all points are abusing.

There are many kinds of abuse that don't seem abusive by the culture's definition. Passive aggression may be difficult to identify. A client's husband pulled up her beloved tomato plants before the season was over. When he said that they would die soon anyway, she sensed it was a cover for expressing aggression in an unrecognizable way.

Other kinds of hurtful actions are invisible because they are within the culture's definition of acceptable, and difficult to describe because cultural denial prevents their being noticed. So getting together in a group to watch movies and TV ads, stopping each minute to examine the exchanges for shaming, is needed in order to remove denial from what is going on all the time. TV ads typically shame someone.

While I was checking out in a pet store, the manager spoke to the checker in a cold and critical tone. I am sure she would have denied she was shaming. She saw herself as a powerful supervisor giving needed information to an underling. The underling hated her and hid it well. Though this situation would be considered by many as harsh, others would think the manager was doing a good job and would assume that the checker deserved it. Before studying shame I would have thought the manager was not very nice, but acting within the norm for her position.

Anytime people are in an abuser stance, they are shaming others.

All abuse is shaming. Those who have healed sufficiently can observe abuse without receiving shame. But for every person who has internalized shame - everyone - abuse elicits our belief that there is something wrong with us. If we as babies believed we were neglected because of who we are, this same belief will be present in later abuses. Women who are hit and controlled have to struggle to believe that they don't deserve such treatment. Men who are shamed for not doing things correctly will believe the criticism, even while disbelieving it. Both partners then defend against their own shame by shaming the other. Thus is born the circular argument, going around and around with no idea of the original subject. The subject isn't important. The shaming style of the argument is.

Manipulating and controlling others can be difficult to perceive as abuse. A man told his wife that she was controlling when she refused to go sailing with him on a weekend that she chose to spend otherwise. He said that

61

because she wouldn't let him do what he wanted, she was controlling him. The truth is that he was controlling her. He wanted her to do what he wanted instead of respecting her own use of time. By getting her to believe that she was doing something harmful he controlled her. Over the course of the day as they sailed, she felt resentful, refused to crew, and sulked. She couldn't see that he was abusing by convincing her that she was shame-worthy. Yet she knew the truth on some level because she took it out on him. She shamed him in return.

For this woman to have stayed out of this morass, she would have to see that setting boundaries is not controlling. She'd have to see the false reasoning was to control her. If she had known that she was going to make him pay with her attitude, she might have gained the strength to not let him. Even if he were to shame her more, and punish her in some way, she'd experience less shame than what she brought on herself by going along with his shaming, and then making him pay for it.

Being Seen by Co-Healers

Studying together with others provides the support of being seen by several people at the same time. In a grocery store when a mother is yelling shaming comments at a child, we are pretty sure that she is hurting him. But no one says anything. The closest people come is to make quiet, side comments to another shopper. While this may peel away some denial, it continues the sense that this is normal. "Oh my god, look what this terrible person is doing to her child! We aren't like that, are we? I know you aren't, and you can see that I'm not."

What would it take to truly see that this mother is at her wits' end, she just can't think clearly or care anymore about how she appears? This kid is driving her crazy.

Our culture has a rule that we aren't allowed to speak to the mother. The only exception is attacking her.

One man who did was, of course, yelling at his own mother for when he was a child. The woman he told to stop talking that way to her child was with a friend, and they both looked at him as if he was crazy. Other shoppers took his side. Nothing in the child's life changed.

Imagine speaking to the mother. If you were able to observe, to see that she is full of shame, that she has passed this along to the child who now drives her nuts, and that she can't change herself to be a non-shaming mother, then what? Intervening is useless. The child has been harmed, and he will continue to be. There is nothing you can do to help him.

We all need to cry for the shame that has dominated each of us and the sadly limited world we live in.

Perhaps it can help to know that grief and evolving out of a shame-based life are what you can do for this child. As each of us purifies ourselves by removing shame, we offer that to everyone around us without saying a word. I can imagine standing and looking at this mother. No smile. Just looking. Reflecting what I see with compassion. Not shaming her.

She will feel probably feel more shame if I do this. But I didn't cause this shame. It is layers upon layers of old shame that she is, for a moment, not masking. She may receive no benefit, but I will get to live in the truth.

I know that she can't help it, that she needs assistance to heal her shame, that she is programmed by the culture and her family's history to take it out on the next generation. She is carrying it forward. For a moment she will be in the presence of someone who is no longer carrying it on. She has a mirror available of who she really is. I cannot determine if she will use that mirror. All of us who are healing shame can offer up a new view, though. As more and more of us become able to do this, more and more people around us will, too - even without setting out to. We are creating a movement. It is all we can do. It is all we need to do.

Rescuer Position in the Triangle

Since rescuing seems to be a very nice thing to do, it is a popular choice for those who work to avoid shame, who want to prove that shame isn't warranted.

In contrast to meeting real needs and giving loving gifts, the rescue position in the triangle sets up the giver and the receiver to believe that something real and nice is going on. However, giving for the wrong reason shames the receiver.

Here are some examples:

A man projects a childhood need for constant attention, and shames his wife if she doesn't meet it. This need isn't real. It isn't true in the present. He didn't receive attention when needed in childhood, and all he can do now is grieve for the deprivation.

His wife will try to meet his expressed need for attention and concern though it can't be met. This is a set-up for issues where one member actually tries to do what the mother of the infant had not, instead of learning to differentiate what is truly needed in the present.

Some professions have a high percentage of people who feel good about themselves for being able to help. This goes beyond meeting real needs and experiencing the inherent pleasure in doing so. When these helping professions attract people who need to feel good about themselves to offset shame, much of the motivation and pleasure comes from reducing shame. And much of the "help" isn't what the patient needs, but instead what will make the helper feel good.

Those people who are so very nice, smiling and acting as if you are a good friend when you have just met, are offering a rescuer false self. The client who spoke lovingly of his father and brothers, effusing over how important they are to him, then revealed that he spoke with his brothers only on holidays and birthdays, and his father on a monthly schedule. After his mother left when he was five he was the family rescuer. His rescuer emotions continued even though he stopped the behaviors.

My mother spoke warmly with a smile to all people, then immediately criticized them behind their backs. Many actually thought she cared for them.

A friend has a brother who spends a lot of time in victim, lamenting how his mother violated his childhood, and that the world is against him. When his sister responds as if she can help him, she gets frustrated because she fails to rescue. When she offers help to friends and to me it is powerful, and full of love. That's because we can accept real help while her brother can only ask for victim rescue.

From the time she was a small child a client was trained by both parents to rescue them. They acted helpless and needy, and made her feel guilty if she didn't put their needs first. Guilt played in her adult life, as she believed that rescuing her husband and friends was the only way to be of value. She found it difficult to fend off guilt when becoming boundaried and meeting only real needs because both parents had done such a thorough job. First she had to stop rescuing them. Both had homes, jobs, friends and social lives. It was difficult to grasp that taking a rescuer stance with these adults, now in their 60's, was actually putting them down because it was based on the assumption that they couldn't take care of themselves. They, too, believed that they couldn't, even while both did.

Lisa learned to rescue because it was the only way she got attention from her mother and grandmother. It worked when natural ways weren't effective. Although neither woman was able to openly love her, they did appreciate when Lisa served them. She discovered what both women liked, and offered it as often as it could be received.

As the mother of adult children, Lisa believed for a long time that her value was to give and give. This is a classic example of projecting what was true, or believed to be true, in childhood onto one's adult life. Of course rescuing her children wasn't what they needed, but Lisa operated on what had gone on in the past. It took years of therapy to realize that she was lovable and loving, and that these qualities hold far more value.

As her shame and trauma healing progressed, she came to see that it wasn't loving to give money, things and time to reduce her shame. Gradually she realized that telling them the truth, responding to their real needs in ways that felt good to her, and setting clear boundaries was really loving them. She is becoming clear about the difference between rescue and meeting real needs, but occasionally finds herself angry when they imply that she isn't caring when she sets a boundary.

Lisa's rescue behaviors helped her feel like a good person because her mother and grandmother only saw her as valuable when she served them.

Rescue by not Telling the Whole Truth

When we hold back information because we don't want to hurt someone's feelings, we are operating on conditioning from childhood and the culture. Deciding that the other person can't handle a situation when he or she really can, is shaming.

Sometimes a rescuer needs to rescue even when the other person doesn't initiate it. For example, the man at the Mexican restaurant who assured me it was okay that I had spilled salsa, and that he would clean it up, thought he was taking care of my shame. But I had no shame. He couldn't see that because he enjoyed being a rescuer. Before I understood this behavior, I would have been defensive, wanting to tell him to just clean it up, don't ingratiate himself to me like that. Since defensiveness is a reaction to shame, I knew that this is what I had felt in the past. Not being perceived accurately brought on shame. He didn't know that I was capable of spilling salsa and not feeling apologetic about it.

My reaction makes sense when I think about how babies need to be seen correctly in order to experience themselves accurately. Now that I can observe what is going on, I can avoid wasting my time with shame and the defense against it.

Any time a person is in a rescuer stance, he is shaming others. This is because he is implying that you can't manage something yourself, that you are too weak or poor or helpless or shame-ridden.

I have found that learning to recognize when others are rescuing, and when they are meeting real needs, has been difficult. With so many people out of touch with real needs, and seeing which ones are false, it can be confusing to differentiate.

Subtle Shame

Facial expressions can communicate a great deal. By the way, Botox inhibits facial expressions so that people can not communicate shaming in the same way.

Even shaming that is strikingly obvious is invisible until denial is lifted. Facial and body expressions carry shame. Some people express shame in their facial expressions in order to prevent others from delivering more. If someone looks embarrassed as a way of life, we are likely to rescue them by not adding more.

A man's picture on a website had a smile that was more of a grimace, his mouth held tightly. Asking myself how I would respond if he were in front of me, I think I would tend to smile reassuringly, let him know that I won't hurt him and not to worry. My rescue patterns are still sufficiently active that his facial request to not shame him could work even on me, someone who has studied these communications for a long time.

I know a man who has a shameful expression, makes hesitant sounds and exhibits uncomfortable body movements. He talks about how he is valued for his business acumen and how he can figure things out. The communication is clear. He wants others to tell him how he is good, smart, clever, helpful so that he can feel good about himself. If you encountered such a person, wouldn't you want to help him offset his shame?

When learning to recognize shaming, looking at pictures in magazines can help. While I wrote books on sexuality, I collected pictures of people looking sexy in a manner that the culture defines as not sexual. One picture showed a woman broadcasting sexual energy while holding a young boy against her breast. He looks stricken, yet this picture was used in full-page, glossy magazine ads.

Pictures on magazine covers on newsstands and in grocery stores reveal shaming. After studying Cosmopolitan covers for months I could see that many models' typical expressions were shaming. Sexual shaming. Women are invited to join the model in putting men down.

Some glamour pictures portray helpless women, hoping you will find them attractive. These are the typical object of some sex addicts who know which women cannot say no. I invite clients to bring in family pictures so I can point out expressions. Noticing the expressions of strangers may be easier than discovering those of people you know, in particular, your family.

Humor

Humor can effectively stop the feeling of shame. It might be self deprecating to communicate to others that you already feel shame, and so they don't need to shame you.

After playing racquetball, my partner and I were sitting outside the court when two men went in to play. After a minute they came out and asked us about the rules because they hadn't played for twenty years. As they asked, they laughed! What could have just been questions and answers became laughing at themselves for having to ask. We laughed along with them, tacitly agreeing that this was indeed shameful, but we would make light of it.

I found it intriguing that when we ran into each other over the weeks, we all greeted each other warmly as if we had a bond from that exchange. The humor meant we had shared something special.

Once I was aware that I used humor to diminish shame, it became a wonderful signal! When I hear my laugh, I stop myself, say that was shame, and speak again in a straightforward manner. Not only do I stop avoiding shame, I obtain a rapid education about what I have shame about. For example, when I laughed over relying on my intuition, I stopped myself. Yes, I do this unusual reading of people. That's a fact. It's not a cause for embarrassment. It isn't a reason to communicate, "Aren't-I-strange," inviting my guest to assure me that she doesn't care.

After many of these examinations, I started naming what would have been self-shaming. When I didn't sweep the cat hair off the floor, I told my friend that the old rules said I should have, or else done a humor-based apology. I said that it wasn't time for me to want the floor swept based on my own cat hair limits, but if she had a need for my house to be cleaner, I would be glad to do that - for her. This was about facts, not about rules for homes and for shame about them. If a visitor is uncomfortable with clutter or cat hair, I will take care of it. But not because of shame!

Using humor when telling stories of failure can offset shame. Self-deprecating humor is a way to become congruent with the shame in order to not feel it. The advice to laugh at yourself is really about avoiding shame. The statement that you shouldn't take yourself so seriously is telling you to stop exhibiting shame.

Poor Boundaries

When employees, friends and relatives have difficulty naming their boundaries, they may feel like blaming you for not knowing. This is a form of shaming. They are likely to tell you that you should have known, or been considerate. Even if they take responsibility, just their cautious reaction conveys that you are causing them problems. If you are seen as a problem causer, you are seen as shame-worthy.

The boss tells the assistant that he wants her to find a caterer for a large meeting he is having over lunch. He explains that he wants nice plates and serving ware, not wrapped sandwiches. She looks at him with concern, as she has never interacted with caterers, and doesn't know how to find one, particularly a good one. She stands there with a concerned look on her face, but is afraid tell him. Inside she is saying this isn't in her job description, he should do it himself, he should find someone else to do it, why does he have a formal lunch meeting anyway? He should just take them all out to a nice restaurant. She sees herself as one down, he is one up. From this stance she can only see him as a demanding boss.

He can tell that she is shaming him, but doesn't know why. He reacts by giving her more detailed instructions. He wants to fire her. He doesn't like having an employee who acts as if he is abusing her.

If she were able to tell him that she knows nothing about this, then he could either instruct her or find an alternative. They would be equals. They could work it out together.

Because we live in a hierarchic world, this kind of scene is a common source of invisible shaming. Students obey teachers, and resent them for it. Resentment is shaming. Equality between the sexes continues to increase, but still women give too much power to husbands, and then resent them for it.

Shaming and Boundaries

Mental health authors reveal the need for boundaries in order to have good relationships and powerful lives. Shame brings many to fear having boundaries, because they don't feel deserving. Others over-set boundaries, and use control to get what they want. Few have so little shame that comfortably doing what is right, and communicating it, is easy. These are people who have probably done some healing.

Lying is an easy indicator of lack of boundary-setting. The popular TV show, Frasier, used lying as a common disrupter. Family members were unable to tell each other what they wanted, or what they were doing to avoid being shamed, and so lied about it. Of course, by the end of the show they had been caught or confessed.

When you study shame, notice lying. It can be fruitful to tell your stories of growing up with adults lying, and how you lied because boundaries weren't respected. For example, children say they didn't do something in order to avoid being punished. Perhaps you continued even when you no longer needed to. If you can set aside shame for lying, then you get to discover why you felt the need to use it to set boundaries.

Most of my male clients' wives shamed them, and because they didn't realize it wasn't appropriate, they took it. But they hated taking it, so made their wife pay by having sex outside the marriage, and lying. Then they felt worse about themselves, and believed the shaming was appropriate. And around and around. These men didn't believe they had the right to limit how they were treated, and weren't able to be shamed without taking it in.

I wrote most of this book in several Starbucks, listening in on conversations. I watched the many ways people reveal their internalized shame and how they shame each other. Try this in restaurants and coffee shops. Listen to voices. Notice reactions to subtle shaming. Does the recipient shame back, become controlling, become silent? Act like nothing happened?

Defensiveness

The next chapter, Shaming in Self Defense, addresses the defensive response to shaming. This response is the most culturally approved and culturally denied. When observing a friend being shamed, one may defensively take her side. That other person is wrong wrong wrong! Without recognizing when we feel defensive, or when others do, we are hampered in healing.

Becoming defensive is a guaranteed signal that shame is felt. The circular arguments of couples, where they shame each other around and around, are examples of defensive responses to the other, followed by attack. I didn't do it, it wasn't my fault, you did something worse, you never approve of me, who do you think you are, why do you always treat me like this?

Many are triggered even by healthy anger and constructive criticism. Even more comes from unhealthy anger and unconstructive criticism. People dance around each other as they try to not feel shame.

One client was able to be calm when attacked. After more than a year of therapy he was in a situation as a first responder, and one of the people began criticizing him harshly. In the past my client would have attacked back, feeling righteously justified in raging at someone who started it. But this time, with his shame level greatly reduced, as the man snarled, he became increasingly calm. When the attacker paused, my client asked if there was anything more they could do for him. He said no, so my client proceeded to leave.

This client had healed from taking responsibility for anything disruptive, shaming himself for not making things go correctly, and reacting with irrational anger. As he progressed through his healing, his shame dropped. He said that he couldn't even remember what it was like to rage back. This gave him freedom to see when his wife didn't support the marriage because he no longer reacted with raging. He could calmly see. And then name his boundaries.

Disagreement, explaining why a comment is incorrect, and saying that this kind of treatment needs to stop can be done without shaming. It is possible to assess and respond with no emotion. When feeling shame, the first reaction is to defend oneself.

Studying Defensiveness

Defensiveness is typically a reaction to the experience of shame.

It might help to know that every single person gets defensive! Because of this, it seems like a normal human reaction.

You feel it. Notice the physical sensation of stomach tightening, of anger, of questioning how this could be happening. Defensiveness is very unpleasant because it's an attempt to defend against the emotion of shame by proving that it isn't appropriate to feel. The truth is, yes it isn't appropriate to feel toxic shame! But the person well trained with shame can't believe that, and struggles to be seen as right, as not harmful, as not stupid.

Although studying one's own defensiveness is a long-term project, it can be quite simple to begin noticing it in others! It goes on everywhere. When I ask the person bagging my groceries to put them in fewer bags, I can be met with defensiveness, as if I were saying he is doing it wrong. Some people at coffee shops can feel mildly defensive over having to give their order. I wonder if they fear they aren't doing it right, or worry that any hesitation or awkwardness will be a bother. They may turn it on the coffee shop as doing something wrong by having so many choices.

Defensiveness can be seen in posture, and in a pulling in of energy, a holding back, a hesitation. Frowns and puzzled expressions.

Movies and TV are full of hatred carried to the extreme of violence. Instead of joining the characters in justifying their hatred, step back and examine why they feel it. What does it do for them? What would they feel if they didn't feel hate? How would they have handled the situation differently? How much of the hate brought the desire for revenge? How much pleasure do you receive from joining them in revenge? How are the writers and directors and actors getting us to feel hatred and revenge in order to avoid our own shame? How do they set out to intensify emotions when bringing a group of people together? Movies in a theater will take us out of our ordinary, shame-filled lives and give us a break by having made-up feelings. For a while.

Chapter 4: Shaming in Self Defense

Avoiding Triggering Others' Shame

Everyone hates feeling shame. Many hate to trigger shame in others because of knowing how bad it feels. And we want to avoid that person shaming us for shaming them.

One outcome of this avoidance comes when people have difficulty setting boundaries. If someone calls for a long talk, and you prefer to finish your project and talk later, you must declare that with a sense of apology, communicating that you really want to talk, please don't be mad. You know that if cut off, the caller may feel rejected or unloved, the experience of shame. And then shame you.

Helping Others Avoid Feeling Shame

We don't want them to feel this kind of pain, and we don't want them to defend themselves because it might include attacking us. We smile, feign interest, don't set limits, act nice, helpful, agreeable, and use other methods to inhibit another's experience of shame.

The exception occurs in marriages and other relationships when anger appears. Then a spouse may tell the other person what is wrong with them. When the person feels shamed, they are likely to become defensive, and attach back. The nature of circular arguments.

Defending Ourselves

When shamed we can accept the shame and feel badly, or defend against it. Shame-free people aren't defensive because they don't need to defend themselves against shame.

Many people are lying in wait for shame to be directed at them. Someone who expects to be shamed won't be able to tell the difference between shaming and information. For example, if I tell someone who has been consistently ten minutes late that I would like him to come on time, I am likely to be met with long, defensive explanations. Or long apologies.

Couples engaging in circular arguments are defending against the partner's defending. It goes around and around. Many clients respond defensively to everything their spouse says. It becomes a lifestyle. While this may avoid feeling shame, it creates a victim mentality. The men feel perpetually victimized, and resist. Their shame prevents them from setting boundaries with their wives, or even seeing when she is not shaming.

Society supports the belief that men are bad. Women are the good gender, doing no wrong while men are the crude, obnoxious, abusive ones. Men often have an easier time getting started in couples therapy because they already think they are bad. I get to help them relieve shame in order to see what they really want to change. Women come in with complaints about others, and because they are defined as good, have more difficulty in seeing how they are harmful. Shame is more painful for women because it has been more completely denied, and then not felt. Women can defend against feeling bad by seeing men as the bad ones. Men agree.

Shaming Others

The woman who talked compulsively about how not playing racquetball wasn't personal brought out my shaming. I didn't say anything, but inside I was thinking, "Really, how stupid to think I would take it personally; listen, just stop and let me get onto the court." When I can't set boundaries, such as walking away in mid-sentence, I lapse into wanting to shame.

Shame-based defensiveness is seen in the tone and facial expression that says no, you're wrong, I'm not bad! It includes the victim presentation of, you hurt me, I've been wronged, it isn't fair, they are out to get me. These bad feelings invite the listener to rescue in order to feel like a good person, relieving her own experience of shame for a time.

I referred a client to an addictions treatment program and when the therapist there called me she described him in a shaming tone, as if he were a difficult person. I had carried a remote belief that treatment program professionals wouldn't do this. After all, these are the very programs that help people heal shame!

Here' a nice example. I drove through a parking lot where two streets intersect, with only one stop sign. As I approached, the car that was stopped at the sign started driving. He obviously thought I had a stop sign, too. I started to get annoyed, shaming him for breaking the rules, when I realized that he didn't know. He had made a mistake. If I had grown up in a shame-free community I would never have had to think about it. All of us would understand that no one is perfect, and we would work together to get everyone through the intersection. There would be no need for comments such as, "Hey, get out of my way!" or "Sorry, I didn't see that you had no stop sign," or "That's okay, don't worry about it."

While writing books on sexuality, I was frequently attacked. I gave a workshop at a conference, and afterwards almost all of the thirty five to forty participants came up to me to thank me for the way I addressed sexual addiction. However, when I was sent a "representative" sample of attendee evaluations, they were all negative! Shaming still felt good then, and, enraged, I told a lot of others, inviting them to triangulate with me against the leader of the conference. He was the actual person who didn't like what I said.

Now I can smile, knowing that my subject was controversial then, and guess that the conference promoter was a sex addict himself. The world is full of people who were so shamed and harmed in childhood that of course they will see a subject through their distortions. What a waste to become negatively charged and find someone to blame! Really, it's rather entertaining. When members of my professional listserv write madly about discrimination against our understanding of sexuality and healing, I sometimes point out that controversy is really good as it is getting people's attention! I really mean it! What a change for me!

Shaming Spouses to Avoid Self-Hate

Spouses and children are the easiest scapegoats in order to stop that dreadful feeling of self-hate. Many of my clients have discovered that when shame begins to emerge, they are likely to pick a fight with their spouses. They do this by criticizing. One woman would return repeatedly to the subject of her husband's infidelity and want him to move out. This alternated with loving and appreciating him. When she was self-hating, nothing would convince her that she didn't truly need him to leave.

Shame is such a terrible feeling that methods to avoid it can be rationalized as real. I often cannot convince someone that they are responding to shame, and to memory, even when they have been through it many times before.

Shame-based attacks on spouses may include physical violence, critical comments, threats of divorce, anger over mild transgressions, attempts to control, lying, and making circular arguments. These arguments begin with something so minor, neither can remember what it was by the time they are in my office. One person starts, the second reacts defensively (shame-induced), then the first reacts defensively. Each attacks in order to defend himself or herself. If neither felt shame the discussion would have begun and ended quickly. Circular arguments indicate that shame is interfering with relating.

Lisa's experiences in childhood demonstrate how internalized shame early in life interferes with healthy marriages. After shame coming from rejection, sexual abuse, depression and consequent poor performance in school, she chose men like her abusive father. She entered that bizarre situation in which she shamed the man, believing that he warranted it because he was abusive. If she had been able to set boundaries, she would have been healthy enough to not have entered this relationship in the first place.

Pregnant with her first baby, she criticized Rob for not showing interest in the pregnancy. Then after giving birth, for having no interest in preparing homemade baby food. When he no longer found her sexually appealing she shamed him for that.

Rob took on this shaming, as men do. But he hated her for it, and expressed it in passive-aggressive ways. He would be late, forget to buy something she needed, or insist on the TV being loud. He received shaming for this, too, and gradually became more overt in his retaliation. When he lost control and hit her, she decided that he was truly a bad person. Her family and his aligned with her against him. No one understood how her shaming contributed to the nightmare. They divorced soon after.

When Lisa started therapy during her second marriage she learned that she picked sexually addicted men who could become violently angry. She worked on how she shamed them for their behaviors. When she was able to see her husband clearly, and accept him for who he was, she stopped shaming him. Once she gave up the tight bond that came from the back and forth abuse, she saw that he wasn't open to changing, and she was able to leave.

Defensive or Curious

Defensiveness is a shame-based reaction to feeling shame. If you weren't defensive, you would understand a shaming comment as a reflection of something going on with the other person.

If curious, you would want to know what he didn't like. You would evaluate his response and apologize, or explain how he misunderstood, or see that his objections aren't warranted and do nothing. Curiosity is a shame-free feeling! It feels so much better than defensiveness. I practice noticing when I feel defensive, and instead try on curiosity. When I succeed, it's amazing! I can stop the shutting down that comes with shame-based anger.

If someone abruptly says something like "What do you want?" he is in a bad mood, and you happen to be in front of him. Yet most people would join you in feeling angry and defensive about his rudeness.

Calling him rude allows you to feel less shame.

If you had no shame you could see that he is not a happy person and it isn't personal. We need to educate ourselves about small examples of defensiveness so we can become aware of our own shame.

As my informal shame study continued, I discovered that I could see my shame-laced patterns more and more clearly. When talking with a friend, I heard myself tell her in an apologetic tone that I thought I had told her this before. I don't need to apologize. I am going to tell her again anyway, so why mention the possibility that I had said it before? In the past I played out these patterns, and then apologized for having the pattern! What a waste of time and energy. This is changing as my awareness has sharpened. I don't have to do anything more than just become aware. Change follows in its own time.

Examples of defensive shame

1) Her: You were an hour late, what's up?

Him in shame: Well, it wasn't my fault, the traffic was terrible and I had to stop for gas, I couldn't help it. You're always after me. I didn't do anything wrong.

Him out of shame: Yes, I am. I tried to call but my phone didn't go through. I'm sorry you had to wonder.

2) Him: I saw you flirting with another man. You hurt me.

Her in shame: What are you talking about, I wasn't flirting. I was just being friendly. I don't have any interest in him, what's wrong with you, you always think I'm after someone. You don't trust me.

Her out of shame: I was, wasn't I? I see how that hurt you. It isn't right to flirt when I'm in a relationship.

3) Him: You're not telling me the truth. You said you were at your friend's and I was told you were at a bar. Why did you lie?

Her in shame: What are you doing checking up on me? Don't you trust me? You never believe me, why should I bother telling you the truth? You wouldn't believe the truth either. (Name calling is frequent here).

Her out of shame: Yes. I lied. (pause) I think I was afraid you would judge me for having a drink with a friend and not inviting you. I shouldn't have lied. I'm glad you told me.

The Difference Between Shame and Anger

Angry shaming isn't a valid expression of anger, and won't discharge it. It is another defense used to avoid feeling one's own shame. Healthy anger meets a real need. Shaming doesn't. Healthy anger is straightforward, focused on the anger itself, with the intent of getting it out. Angry shaming uses a put down tone, and is focused on the other person. Regardless of the words, it communicates that the other person has done something seriously wrong.

Being Acceptable May or May Not Be Shame-Based

Our natural human motivation includes wanting to be acceptable to the community and to fit in. The healthy function of shame includes this, because it supports the development of community. Toxic shame distorted this into the belief that we will or will not be allowed to belong. In a shame-based culture we can only really fit in if we share the same rules for how to function.

When heavily in avoidant attachment, I couldn't fit in. Or if I did, I didn't experience it. Now that I am healing shame and relinquishing my need for separation, I find that there are wonderful ways to fit in that don't require following the rules of those I fit in with! Healing shame makes it possible to live well and fit in from a gentle, inwardly directed existence.

Non-Shame-Based Emotions

As human creatures, we come with the capacity to experience a range of emotions. All can be healthy expressions of our community-based nature. And all can become distorted from living in a shame-based culture.

Day-to-day life includes fear of feeling shame. However, some fear is not shame-based. Real fear, from narrowly avoiding a car accident, or seeing a child run into the street, is useful for staying alive and keeping the species going. During a recession, fear can assist taking steps to be safe. Fear from childhood or adult trauma may not be shame-based, even though from the perspective of the present, it is irrational. The well-known flashbacks of combat vets also occur for people who have been abused in the past.

Shame-based fear makes up most of the fear that humans experience. What a waste of time, energy, adrenal function, and life!

Shame can change the experience of hurt, too. Hurt is a real feeling when one's monogamously bonded partner is sexual with others. Hurt alerts the betrayed one. When this hurt is expressed it can alert the betrayer that their activity is harmful. Like healthy shame and anger, it is a signal that integrity is off and something needs to change. But when the betrayed person adds shame to the hurt, it becomes difficult to heal. The hurt can go on and on even when its purpose has been served.

Anger is a powerful boundary-setter. When the other person doesn't respond to a calm statement of a limit, anger can become necessary to get his or her attention. The extreme is seen in wars. In shame-free cultures, war would not be necessary because conflicts would be worked out.

In our culture, anger occurs most often as a defense against shame. People who talk down to others, who control with the power of being a boss or with money, who shame others for not seeing things their way, trigger anger. If we had no shame we would shake our heads and walk away when others want to shame. Psychotherapy clients love when they can finally stop reacting to a parent or spouse or boss.

Laughter is a wonderful emotion and very good for our physiology. But based on shaming, or being shamed, or making unhealthy jokes, it becomes a defense against shame. Laughing at oneself is a culturally accepted way of stopping the experience of shame. Other people will laugh at you good heartedly, too, in order to help you stop feeling shame.

Flirting is an energizing experience for single people who want to communicate an attraction to someone who is also available. This is a healthy use of sexual energy. However, flirting is commonly used to create an intensity that can't progress into romantic relating. This meaningless interest is employed to reduce the experience of shame because flirting implies that the recipient is attractive and valued. When the flirter then flirts with someone else, the recipient becomes angry or hurt, having lost the source of feeling valued, thus avoiding shame.

Even contentment or peace or satisfaction can be created in order to avoid the feeling of shame. For example, if you believe that someone is critical of you, or you are about to be sanctioned at work, learning that you are wrong feels good. The shame disappears. Social drinking can create false positive emotions, and permit a more enjoyable evening because alcohol reduces the experience of shame.

Recognizing Why Others Act the Way They Do

We are all confronted by others' strange behaviors, such as intense criticism, attack, withdrawal, denial of a problem obvious to everyone else, etc. If we can remember that irrational behaviors are the result of fear or shame, it is easier to understand what is going on. When you take it personally, all you can do is make up the other person's motivation. It is actually very simple. He or she is reacting to their feelings of shame in the form of low self-esteem, their need to turn it on others, and more.

We encounter other people's defenses against feeling shame. The next chapter covers the numerous ways we inhibit our own feeling of shame.

Chapter 5: Sexual Shame

Most people are aware of having shame around sex. My work with sexual abuse survivors and sex addicts made it clear that shame underlies the issues for both, and impedes healing. I wrote about this in a book called Treating Sexual Shame.

Sexual shaming is unavoidable.

Sexual shaming is universal, incorporated into the culture. Even when parents try their best to talk openly with children, they cannot have healed their own sufficiently to not pass some of it on. Even if parents do a fairly good job, peers pass along the shame they received. When figuring out how to date and kiss and engage sexually, children do not have good role models. They are left with rules from adults, unspoken beliefs of parents, and pressure from peers.

Every one of us had shameful sexuality directed at us by television, jokes, high school classmates making lewd comments, gestures and sounds, and the Internet. Looking at pornography shames the viewer because the culture says it is shameful. And, the actors are conveying "dirty" or "bad" behaviors, as shame has become part of what is arousing. The shame of pornography adds to the shame already in place, cementing it.

Anyone who wishes to heal must address sexual shame that violates our basic humanness.

Shaming from Sexual Abuse

Sexual abuse victims take on the shame of their abusers during the molestation or rape. The pedophile or sex addict or anyone who crosses sexual boundaries feels shame because the whole culture condemns what they are doing. When overriding shame, they are able to carry out acts that violate their integrity, but their shame is energetically transmitted to the child.

The child's own shame about sexuality is already in place before the molestation, which compounds the shame from the act. When the molester approaches the child, the child has already associated shame with the attitude of the adult. In the same manner that babies interpret lack of love and attention as meaning something about their own worth and lovability, molested children usually interpret the sexual attention as something they have caused or initiated or agreed to. The molested child's shame is magnified.

We therapists have repeatedly heard how incest survivors weren't able to tell their parents or other adults. We have also heard mothers lament over why the child didn't tell, assuring her or him that she would have stopped the abuse.

The child's sexual shame level was so high that she couldn't reveal this shameful experience. Even though it was done to her, the shame is still there. Imagine what it would be like as an adult to describe to your mother the experience of oral sex. Every client I ask about sexual activity is embarrassed, even though they know I specialize and so have heard it all. Most were unable to talk with other therapists, needing a specialist in order to override shame. Then add to this the horror of truly shameful sexual behavior, and it becomes impossible for most children to talk to a parent.

When people are in therapy to heal sexual shame, they usually have difficulty addressing what was done to them. It is easier to remember and process beatings and controlling and criticism. These bring shame too, but the level of sexual shame added to already existing sexual shame is overwhelming. In addition, if the therapist isn't paying attention to the shame level, educating the client about this major obstacle to healing, and assisting in the reduction, healing can go very slowly. I have long valued holding workshops on sexual shame because it is brought to the forefront. People can focus on this most inhibiting experience more easily with other people doing the same.

Multiple research studies have long established that about a third of women and a fifth of men have been inappropriately touched as children. We also know that many severe abuses are repressed or denied. Recent studies indicate even higher numbers.

When addressing this deeply felt shame in my sexual shame workshops, women have permission to say nothing. If a woman feels required to talk, her shame could inhibit being able to. At the beginning of a workshop I bring up subjects such as first bras and first kisses and what parents said about sexuality. I tell my own experiences, and this engages others to want to tell theirs. Shame-healing has a natural draw.

Jennifer came to three of my workshops before joining a therapy group. She sat through the first one without speaking. In individual sessions, she cried with amazement over hearing the other women talk about simple things like first menstruation and attraction to boyfriends. She said her heart was frozen, clutched tightly in her chest, even while the other women's eyes got brighter and livelier as the hours went on.

Jennifer had sex from the time she was fifteen but managed to put it into a separate compartment to avoid the shame that appeared when trying to talk about it. Alcohol helped, even though she wasn't an alcoholic.

Jennifer's terror over the emerging shame supported the need for my guideline that no one has to talk. She was able to tell the other women that she was terrified, which helped them understand and not take her silence personally. They also saw that she listened intently.

When Jennifer was finally able to talk, all of us were surprised by the subject that had brought such distress. Until we heard the whole story. When she started her period at age ten, before she had seen the movie about menstruation, she had no idea what the blood on her clothes was. She thought she was bleeding to death. Here's the really shocking part. She couldn't tell her mother! Her very shame at being alive made her believe that her mother would have no interest, do nothing to take care of her, and let her die. Of course her mother wouldn't do any of those things, but Jennifer's experience of being hated and envied so contaminated her self-esteem that she led her life as if needing nothing from her mother. Her sexual shame over the sign that she was becoming a woman was magnified by her perception of her mother's feeling toward her.

I met her mother when she was on a visit. She is a narcissistic woman who could see little beyond herself and her interests. Raising children had to have been challenging as she preferred staying with her own thoughts. Even when the four girls were adults she was unable to see them for who they were. Jennifer became the surrogate mother, taking care of the younger three so their mother wouldn't feel burdened. Yet in this, too, she was seen as a failure.

Jennifer's mother viewed herself as a powerful woman, and in her 70's when we met, she walked with a sense of dignity and strength. Initially this was appealing until it became clear that she was unable to relate intimately at all. Her facial expression of interest in me appeared feigned. I do believe that she had as much interest as she is capable.

The price of narcissism is an inability to be interested in others. With this disability, she had to come up with logical reasons why her children did what they did. She had no intuitive understanding. Then, sadly, the children made up that their mother's reactions to them is because of who they were.

This client's story demonstrated the importance of siblings when parents can't love adequately. Jennifer became the parent of girls only two, three, and five years younger than she was, because this was valued by them and their mother. With sexuality already distorted in the family, and the younger girls learning about it from an immature older girl, sexual shame and misinformation were rampant.

When exploring why a workshop on sexual shame seemed the best course, Jennifer explained that her self-hate revolved around sexuality. Her mother wanted to be the only beautiful female. She flirted with the girls' boyfriends. She shamed them for any evidence of sexuality.

Passed Along Shame

Sexual shame is the most obvious example of passed-along shame. Parents' discomfort with sexuality shows up in their difficulty talking with their children, in shaming genital touching, and fostering an overall view that sexuality is bad. The culture contributes with words like nasty and dirty, said in a joking or sexual way.

Men want to heal sexual shame, too. But most have a more difficult time taking a look, because they are culturally trained to think that they should be very sexual and have no problem with it. Sex addicts find it easier to heal because they know they have sexual issues. In group therapy their shame emerges, gets talked about, and discharged.

Given that so many of us had the shame-ridden sexuality of another person projected onto us, healing sexual shame may be a valuable starting place. Jennifer discovered this, and later broadened her explorations to her childhood attachment deprivation.

Chapter 6: Overriding the Experience of Shame

Every single one of us carries shame. Every single one of us uses a variety of methods to not feel it. These avoidance maneuvers prevent us from being truly ourselves and automatically living in our integrity.

These maneuvers are so entrenched in the culture, so integrated into cultural consciousness, that they are difficult to see. I have studied them for a long time, knowing that I had to see them for what they are rather than believe they are normal facets of being human. What people mean by "the human condition" isn't human. It's the response to carrying shame.

Healing the Shame that Binds You (Bradshaw, 2005) goes into detail about the clinical defense mechanisms commonly addressed by psychotherapists. It is a good source for those who want to understand more. It also includes a well outlined presentation of the ways people avoid shame.

Some of us have experienced such abuse and neglect in childhood that we carry a great deal of emotional pain. It is often too much for the culturally approved methods of avoiding shame to handle, and so we are forced to learn how to heal.

Most people live their lives following the rules, proving they are good people, searching for the esteem of others, obtaining approval for who they are. Social drinking makes relating easier, gossip brings a sense of closeness. They can manage their shame by diminishing its intensity.

In the healing of shame, it is vital to observe how you avoid it. If you continue the avoidance, it isn't available to be healed.

When my own practices became obvious, I could decide to stop them. However, other maneuvers only became visible after I had stopped using them! I didn't know they were shame avoiders until I no longer needed them to avoid shame!

And then there are the complicated ones that enhance life while avoiding shame. For example being married. Coupling and having children are obvious human instincts as they have occurred since recorded history, are found in all cultures, and enhance our species survival. Marriage can also manage shame. Those choosing to be unmarried are not obeying the custom, and that can bring a sense of being different, not fitting in – shame fodder.

Then there are those of us who elect avoidant attachment as a way to safely preserve ourselves, yet we still need closeness. Two avoidant attachers can marry, create what looks like a loving, typical family, yet live as emotionally separate as they did when growing up.

When I married I was terrified to go out into the world on my own. I could not imagine a life centered on myself, on my professional interests and preferred living location. I needed someone. This can be seen as just fear, fear of being unable to make a life for myself, shyness that prevents creating a new social life, uncertainty in making good decisions.

My fear was of shame. The nature of this fear is like the fear of public speaking. It is irrational, even while strong and very real. My concern about going out in the world was the same. I could of course do it. I was intelligent, I knew how to apply for jobs I qualified for, I could live with my parents until I could support myself. There was nothing real to fear.

As an avoidant attacher, however, I lived as an alien. When in memory, I didn't know if I could understand what was needed, and then do it. An investment partner and I shared this irrational fear. We were both capable of making good investments, but by doing it together we were able to stay present. It was apparent that by having each other to reflect back to us the integrity of our decisions, we were able to plunge forward into a fascinating business. Our shame was out of the way. When problems came up, we breezed through them. I could see that my partner was in integrity with our decisions, and he could see that I was. As we were able to believe in each other, neither of us felt shame!

After so much healing, I can make these same investments alone. If I hadn't healed sufficiently, I would need to work with someone else to quiet my shame. Why not, when I have a guaranteed method of preventing shame from stopping me from doing something satisfying and lucrative? For the same reason, I often plan exercise that requires setting up appointments. When arranging something with someone else, I am out in the world, in my real present-day life. If I were going out on a walk or bike ride alone, I might still not go. The old view of myself as an alien could re-emerge and prevent me from stepping forward in natural, self-caring ways.

When we feel unable to care for ourselves, to eat and exercise and carry out many easy activities, it is shame-based! This is so common that it is hard to see that it isn't the nature of mankind. Now I know that when I don't take good care of my body, it's caused by shame!

Lisa worked on identifying her shame and how she defended against it. It took a while for her to accept that shaming other people was a ploy to avoid her own shame. Since this was her way to avoid feeling rejectable, unlovable, and unloving, she had to find fault even with a perfect man.

While Lisa used many maneuvers to avoid shame, including being married, condemning men was the most disruptive. Along with many women, she obsessed over what her partner was doing that harmed her. When she criticized him for it, she didn't understand why he grew to hate her. This hatred became the next focus for her condemnation.

As you can see, our methods to avoid feeling shame are complex. They don't fit into a neat list. Each of us must observe ours, allowing them to make sense over time. Many of mine are still not visible, and I have come to see that they may not be until they are no longer needed. I can heal shame without understanding all the ways I avoid it. However, if your defenses do a good job of preventing the experience of shame, you may be served by setting aside one or more in order to see what happens.

Ways We Diminish Feeling Shame

I will describe thirty three acculturated methods of avoiding the experience of shame. There are countless more. Begin with observing. Notice how you avoid feeling badly. Don't demand that you immediately change. Just learn. Just notice.

1. Criticizing

Putting others down. Finding someone else to be worthy of shame makes people feel as if they aren't. Thinking about how bad people are helps them feel as if they are good. Stories on TV magazine shows and talk shows aid viewers in feeling superior by portraying how awful something or someone else is.

2. Alcohol and Drugs

Even in small quantities, drugs and alcohol can alter bad feelings. An everyday example is the small group of people in a restaurant. Often they may be quiet until after their first drink when they become happier and louder. Ordinary shame-ridden people enjoy turning it off for a while.

3. Taking Care of Others

Caregiving to feel like a good person reduces shame. This is in contrast with the innate pleasure of meeting real needs, or agreeing to a division of labor, or conditions of employment. When such actions become habitual shame reducers, they are difficult to recognize for what they are. They can be difficult to confront. After all, how can you question caregiving??

When I was in the hospital I could sense the difference in the attitude of nurses and nursing assistants. Some truly care and haven't lost the ability to perceive what is needed by patients, medically and emotionally. Others act as if they care, but there is no transfer of it to the patient. Still others don't even act like they care, they just do their tasks. The ones who act are probably relieving shame with caretaking.

Those who really seem to care, and perhaps do, may not be responding to real needs. I had an acquaintance who was raised by parents who took turns being sick and being the caretaker. His definition of good people was those who need care and those who take care of others. My acquaintance played this out with his sister after his parents died. In addition to reducing shame, it made him feel as if he belonged. Of course if he were shame-free, or at least had reduced shame, he wouldn't need to make up a way to belong.

4. Religion

Religion can be used to avoid feeling shame. Following rules that are clearly laid out by the highest authority seems to offer security. That is, if the rules can be followed. This backfires because it is hard, if not impossible, to follow all the rules of "goodness."

I believe that we were all born perfectly human and integrated into the big picture of everything. Then shame is laid on the child, beginning with attachment deprivation, followed by cultural shaming, and more.

Because he can't entirely heal, the child becomes to some degree inhuman. This is why children fight, destroy property, compete, demand, bully, act like victims, and so on. Then he must override shame, or heal it, or suffer it. Sadly when religion is used to avoid shame, we can only employ rules for goodness instead of obtaining help with truly discovering our integrity.

Religion can be well used when facing our own defects, and using the wisdom and approaches of the great masters. But it is only a band aid when the guidance is seen as rules to follow.

5. Being Good

Most people try to do the right thing, be considerate, suppress anger, etc., in order to consider themselves "good." Many value a reflection from others that they "have a heart of gold." They are "good people." They "would give you the shirt off their back." This can defend against shame.

A sign on a window of Starbucks said, "Do something good every day." People like a rule or suggestion for how to feel good about themselves! Shame-free people don't need to think about doing something good. They just do good things as a matter of course, without thinking about it. Shame-based people want to think that doing good things makes them good people.

6. Being Really Nice

While all of us have inherent desires to love and be helpful, appearing nice is a classic way for shame-based people to obtain a positive, approving reflection from others. It can be a useful maneuver against shame. Many clients have told me that their abusive fathers were well liked, as if this meant they couldn't really have been abusive.

Bradshaw says that being nice is hostile! It is a manipulation. It uses others. The nice person cannot like having to be nice in order to relieve shame, and is likely to take it out passive-aggressively on those he is nice to.

7. Following Rules

When trying to be good to avoid feelings of shame, a set of rules helps. Following the rules of a church or family or community or sub-culture can make it easier to establish that one is good.

There are no rules for integrity. We each have to heal ours into existence.

8. Rationalizing

All people rationalize their behavior or thoughts in order to justify them as not deserving shame. Typical rationalizations are, it wasn't my fault, he deserved it, he should have known better, he should have done something different, I didn't mean to do it. Or, it's your fault, if you hadn't done that I wouldn't have done what I did, if the laws weren't stupid I wouldn't have broken them.

I am imagining having a party where everyone exaggerates rationalizations they have used or heard, and laughing hysterically! They really are funny if you don't need them or if they aren't directed at you.

9. Psychological Defense Mechanisms

In addition to rationalizing, other psychological defense mechanisms used to avoid shame and other painful experiences include repression of feeling, denial of experience, forgetting something happened, dissociation from all feeling or thought or physical sensation, reaction formation, which is feeling love to override hate, and many more. *Healing the Shame that Binds You* has a longer list with explanations of the use of defense mechanisms.

10. Becoming Congruent with Shame

Some people are so shame-laden that they can't handle it. They may feel relief when becoming congruent with badness. People who cheat, steal, and abuse others are living shamefully, which actually avoids feeling shame. Alcoholics want to be with other heavy drinkers so they won't feel shame. They support each other's use of alcohol. If they drink with non-drinkers, the drinkers' shame will emerge.

Many of my clients had stolen and caused damage when they were teenagers. Teens who feel great shame after years of torment find that "being bad" feels really good. Some parents rationalize that their children got in with the bad crowd, but who are the bad crowd?

Sexual shame is a good example of a universal painful feeling that can be overridden by agreeing that sex is dirty or nasty. Some people are only capable of becoming aroused when they can see sex as dirty or bad. Loving, or "good" sex, can be difficult to engage in. "Bad" sex includes pornography, prostitution, even illicit flirting. Loving, conscious sex brings up the shame that has become attached to sex. I have seen many couples in which the man has no interest in sex with his wife once she stops being willing to act as if it were dirty. This has been called the virgin whore or goddess whore dichotomy. Sex with the "good" woman brings up his shame. Sex with a "bad" woman doesn't, because he becomes congruent with the shame. Healing sexual shame allows people to enjoy loving, healthy sex.

People who override shame with arousal find that orgasm will bring shame back. These are people who can't cuddle afterwards. They have to do something to avoid their discomfort. I had a sexually addicted client who avoided orgasms. He masturbated so much that he would hurt his penis, but he would not have orgasms. He felt terrible when he was not aroused. We learned that he had been severely sexually abused by his father in childhood. This abuse had sexualized him, and shamed sex.

Some people who abuse will later feel shame and remorse, see-sawing back and forth between the two. Others can't tolerate the shame of remorse and are continually controlling of spouses and children and perhaps employees.

Men going out together to strip clubs or looking for one-night stands are supporting each other in being "bad." They are relieved of feeling shame for a little while.

11. Hiding, Concealing, Lying

Deceit is an easy antidote to the fear of receiving shame. Just make something up so the other person thinks you are better than you think you are. Of course, when others discover the lies, far more shame arrives from others and from internalized shame.

Lying develops as a defense against being found out by parents. Once it becomes clear that lying can avoid shame, it becomes a habitual defense. Highly shamed people who needed to lie in childhood can find that they lie with no purpose as adults. It has become habit, much as others habitually smile at everyone. Learning to stop lying can be difficult. First the person has to identify the instances, then notice the intended effect, and then learn what happens when they don't lie.

A friend long engaged in healing lied to me about where she was on the freeway when we were about to meet. Immediately after we got together, she told me. This kept us clear, showing me again that she values honesty, and helped her continue healing from the perceived need to lie.

12. False Self, Clichés

Mental health uses the term, false self, to describe people who have made up their experience so completely that they convey no sense of who they really are or what they are feeling. Some false selves use a series of clichés to communicate so that the listener thinks he or she understands what is being said, but actually doesn't. If you listen closely, you can hear that a series of clichés doesn't really communicate.

When a client talked in a long string of clichés, I came to see that he was unable to do anything else. He was a sex addict who was unable to address his addiction. He could not become vulnerable and give up his methods of medicating shame.

Everyone offers a desirable impression at times, of course. This is because we all carry shame. When the grocery clerk asks me how I am, and I don't answer, she either doesn't notice or thinks I'm strange. She doesn't want to feel shame for asking a question she has no interest in, and having the person respond honestly.

Another sex addict offered a false self that prevented me from grasping his experience of life. He spoke warmly of loving his father, brothers, wife and children, yet I felt nothing. It was like watching bad acting.

He dismissed his sexual activities as being just the way he was, he wasn't harming anyone. When I described his false self he thought I was very strange. After four months I was about to tell him I couldn't see him any more as no therapy was taking place. But then his wife caught him acting out his addiction and told him to move out. He fell apart, became real, and earnestly explored his addiction and the process it served. Over months, he came to discern the components of his false self, and eventually became real most of the time. In fact, he became capable of empathy, of recognizing his intuitive knowing, and of loving in a communing manner. And of course he was much happier. He no longer had to battle the shame of his addiction and the secrecy it required.

13. Unnecessary Apologizing

Apologizing is appropriate when we have done something hurtful. It is our way of acknowledging that we were out of integrity, and see that it was harmful. Healthy shame motivates the apology, and once it is complete, we return to normal.

However, most apologizing isn't truly warranted. The young woman sitting in the big Starbucks chair next to mine moved her things way over to her side of the table between us when I sat down. She said to tell her if she was in my way. This was unneeded because I had far more room than necessary. She put me in a position of forgiving her before she did anything I wouldn't like. This is an effective defense. She prevented me from shaming her, and prevented feeling internalized shame.

An acquaintance communicates by tone, facial expression, and body language that he is always on the verge of feeling shame. He will apologize when what he said wasn't offensive. He gets a de-shame hit. It has nothing to do with the other person. He doesn't even need to be forgiven. Just the act of apologizing is his drug. It does the job.

Notice how you respond when others over-apologize. Do you lean forward and earnestly tell them it's okay? This is what I was to do with the woman sharing a table. This is drug, too.

14. Manipulating and Controlling

Contrast the feeling of being in control and getting others to do what you want with the feeling of being shameful, bad, inadequate, and not worthy of life. If you had to face the second on a regular basis, wouldn't you prefer the first? It feels so much better to think one is knowledgeable and right and powerful.

People who use manipulation as an avoidance maneuver actually bring on more shame because others don't like to be controlled. Many women go to therapy to learn how to set boundaries and refuse control. This is threatening to the controller. If we as a community can understand that people are merely trying to make life manageable, we don't have to shame them for it. Instead, we can just not let them control.

15. Triangulating Against "Bad" People

Feeling like a better person is a common method of avoiding shame. The larger number of people gathering together against a person or a group, the more effective the shame medication. Racism is a good example of large numbers focusing hatred toward another large group. Nationalism is, too, even when other nations are considered allies. Feeling separate, and superior, is useful in avoiding shame. Being part of a community hating a murderer or pedophile together avoids feeling shame. That person is so bad. So much worse than I am.

Politicians, economic leaders, athletes, and celebrities who are doing something that engenders disapproval are put down in a helpless, shaming fashion. Documentaries and news articles exploit this kind of story because it sells. It makes so many people feel good.

16. Gossip

Gossip is the individual, or small-group, form of triangulation. People gossiping together use the emotions of shock, criticism, and shaming to bond with each other. This is a form of trauma bonding, where trauma emotions are used to create bonds when healthier forms aren't available.

Recently a friend invited me to triangulate with him against someone we knew. I wasn't tempted. It alerted me to the very obvious fact that if he enjoys this kind of relating, I will be the object when he does this with others. Isn't it ironic that we think we can be close with someone who interacts in this mode? Gossip is such an integrated facet of American life that even when people intellectually understand that they will also be the object, they don't stop. When they are the object they will feel angry and violated. The roles of gossiper and gossipee are compartmentalized in order to reduce the experience of shame, and isolation, and being left out, and not fitting in.

17. Staying Busy

Being busy is a major, tactic to avoid of shame, popular in our high-speed world. With too much to do and not enough time, there is no room to check inside and see what is going on in there. If you can't check in with yourself, you can't perceive when shame rears up. Busyness can prevent the shame that brings addictive acting out, and the shame that comes after acting out. One can be busy with work, family, and anything else that enables over commitment.

Cell phones, texting, the use of the Internet for electronic games, chat rooms, porn sites and more are all common tools for those who wish to stay away from shame.

18. Romanticizing

Romanticizing might be described as a bright-eyed, sighing exclamation over something seen as really really important. A client said she just knew that in the new year she would become healthy, she would do those prescribed tasks that would finally bring health.

A woman prayed to get a spondee in her 12-step program, and when a woman in the afternoon meeting asked to be her sponsor, the first woman jumped up and down, exclaiming that the second woman made her day. She made up that the prayer and the event meant far more than they do. The reality is that she communicated a readiness for a new experience, and she found that experience. How nice. Her intense reaction was a romanticization of this human event.

Television commercials romanticize. They overdraw the value of what they promote. They attempt to get you to pay more attention, feel good, and thus purchase. Ad creators study people to see what gets attention and cooperation. Advertising might as well say, buy this in order to reduce your shame. Or they entice woman to buy by making the husband look stupid. She gets to shame him by being smarter and purchasing. The vast majority of sales would not take place if we had a shame-free culture.

In a movie a woman told her husband, you will be a wonderful father, and having a baby will be the best thing that could happen to us. Her tone conveyed intensity and drama. She was creating false, romanticized emotions in the present to predict the future.

When romanticizing getting a new job, or into a good college when it happens, it's disappointing to discover that it is just life, just one day after another, and hard work. When we think that the event is the answer, we set ourselves up for disappointment.

This won't occur if we see accurately. We would feel glad for the job or the college acceptance or the spondee, but know that it is only a door into what is possible. Life is only this very day, this moment.

Romanticizing creates a roller coaster of made up-emotion.

19. Broadcasting Sexual Energy

Sexual energy is ours to use when bonding with a partner, for continuing the exclusive bond, and for pleasure in masturbation. Any other transmission, as with revealing clothing, is to obtain reactions from others in order to feel powerful, controlling, attractive, valuable, present, successful, and a host of other antidotes to shame. If someone who is not available flirts with you, there is really no personal interest. This person is using you to feel something about him or herself.

20. Stylized Friendliness

Some people make up a very friendly, interested persona. If you are on the receiving end you might wonder why you don't enjoy such friendly people when they seem so very interested in you. It may be because they are really not interested. They are merely trying to avoid shame.

Some friendly people are very good actors and able to convince you that you truly are interesting. This feels different from the real, less intense, communing interaction that is really human. And truly friendly.

21. Dressing in Style or by the Rules

People spend money and a great deal of time working hard to prove they have no reason to feel shame. Because it is so prevalent, I didn't think much about it until my clients in Southern California started coming to summer sessions wearing calf-high boots lined with fur.

Do many truly dress to feel comfortable? Some might think that people who wear old, torn clothes might be free of social shaming. But they are either rebelling against the rules, or they live in so much shame that it really doesn't matter what they wear. They aren't able to push shame aside with clothing. Taking care of one's body, including putting on clean, neat, attractive clothes, is natural when living shame-free. Choosing lovely colors and textures can be non-shame living.

The phrase, "looking presentable," implies shame if one is not dressed according to societal rules.

22. Being "Beautiful"

Billions of dollars are spent on cosmetic surgery. Research found that breasts created with implants are now considered to be the most sexy. Clothing, working out, hair, makeup, skin treatments, Botox, and surgery are shame reducers for people who think they will be more valuable, and thus have less shame, when they look as good as possible. People rarely succeed because the shame that caused it is still there. With no shame, they wouldn't think that these services added to their value.

23. Trite Explanations of Life

When people say it was meant to be, there's a reason for everything, or it's God's will, they are artificially tidying up their experience. Such explanations take away personal responsibility, and thus personal shame. While these "truths" may be true, speaking them has the function of relieving shame. People can by-pass fear of the consequences of their choices and decisions because these sayings explain anything away. However, they interfere with the grief that is necessary to release past pain in order to live in the present.

The expressions, "making a difference," and "giving back," are romanticized, shame-medicating statements. They are outside-in definitions of goodness. When we are shame-free, we automatically help meet others' real needs, and never even think about it. It feels good because we are community creatures who receive pleasure from living congruently with our nature.

Giving back is based on some kind of record-keeping. I was given to, and so I give to others. Instead, meeting real needs meets a need of ours, and so feels good. Giving back is a distorted view of gratitude, a rule that receiving help must be followed by an appreciative helping back. In a shame-free culture we would all be helping all the time, and we would all be receiving help all the time. It is sad that people can be so cut-off that they resort to a romanticized desire to somehow feel good about themselves.

The goal of helping others becomes part of one's identity of goodness.

If I enjoy helping, I will help. Period

24. Magical Thinking

Creating false beliefs and practices leads people to believe things are true that are not.

When a credit card company lost a class action suit, it sent checks to everyone who had been defrauded by the company. A client, who had borrowed a great deal of money on credit cards to try to handle debt received a sizable check. She told her therapy group that this was evidence she was doing good things, perhaps good work in therapy. She believed that there was a direct connection between getting this money and what she had done. This is a distorted concept of karma, often used as a throw-away reason for many things going wrong. Or right.

Looking for information about what is going to happen, or what one should do, is another area of distortion. A client who believed that bluebirds are a sign of rightness looked out my window to observe a blue jay, and she assumed with a smile that the decision she had been pondering was the right one. When people look for signs, or see signs, they aren't trusting that they already have the information. They may not be able to look within and check out their intuition, their knowing. Shame inhibits it.

25. Develop, or Copy, Values to Live By

When we uncover our natural understanding of being social creatures, knowing how to relate to others is automatic. Healthy shame alerts us if we stray. I want to be honest, respond to real needs of others, work hard for things of value, find my role in the community, develop my abilities and interests and see how they serve, expand myself in whatever ways show up as right for me, learn what integrity is and enjoy operating within it, and much more.

This list might be seen as values to live by, but I just live it, automatically, without thought. I don't do these things because they are good, or because they make me a good person. I do them because that's who I am. My toxic shame hasn't prevented this.

When my mother was in a nursing home, and I held power of attorney, I discovered the difference between accepting responsibility for a parent and providing guilt-ridden attention. By remaining open to this question, I found that I was fully motivated to take care of her finances and make decisions. Every moment felt good with no resentment. However, I didn't visit her to be a good daughter or a good person. My siblings did. I was able to override the voices speaking in my head about what is right. It wasn't right for me to act loving with a parent who had not loved me and who had not received my love. Perhaps it was right for my siblings.

Religion offers rules to follow in order to live up to the values of the culture. Bradshaw uses the term, religiosity, to mean the use of religion to handle shame by following rules and criticizing others for not following them. This is in contrast to using religion to evolve into a less shame-based life.

The term, belief system, has the same quality as values in that it is made up because of having lost the intuitive understanding of how to live. We have to have intellectual beliefs when we don't have access to a natural understanding. Values and belief systems will fall away when they are no longer needed.

You can imagine how awkward it is when someone tells me that I have strong values! I will usually say it isn't a value. I don't have values.

26. Humor Used to Avoid Shame

I watched an old Eddie Murphy video with the audience in hysterics. All he did was say sexual words and walk around the stage, giving permission to people to laugh. I didn't find it funny. I had specialized in sexuality for a long time, and had healed most of my sexual shame. I didn't need humor to hear the words and know what they meant. Sex, elimination, farting, failure, saying the wrong thing, not knowing the answer and so on can be de-shamed with humor.

Writers who say that it is good to be able to laugh at ourselves are referring to self-shaming. We wouldn't laugh at ourselves or others if we didn't need to lighten the feeling of shame. Laughing at ourselves might help while we are learning the causes of our shame and becoming able to see them more clearly. Eventually, freedom from shame would include freedom from laughing at anyone.

When shame isn't limiting us, humor emerges in the simplest activities, expressing the joy of life. The book,

The Continuum Concept, describes men laughing their way through difficult, even painful, physical tasks. Laughter adds energy as controlled out-breathing and moaning allow increased access to physical strength. And it acknowledges that this is a right thing to do even if it is hard.

When playing racquetball with my favorite partner, we laughed our way through the games! When we had a long rally, and getting shots we thought weren't possible, we laughed! We were delighted no matter who got it. When one of us made a bad shot, we didn't laugh at ourselves, we just moved on to the next serve.

27. Greed

Doesn't it make sense that greed would seem like an antidote to being deprived of real love and attention and success and integrity and community and belonging? It can be a search for what one never had. It may seem like a solution to the shame brought about by the deprivation.

Greed seeks to prove that one has worth. It can attempt to prove that you are superior, smarter, better and successful. We see examples of greed that have created great wealth and control over others. Gambling addicts alternate between the ecstasy of seeming to win mommy's attachment and the devastation of losing it. Instead of healing shame, gambling increases it.

28. Falling in Love

If we don't have love all around us naturally, then falling in love holds too much appeal. The cultural draw is intense, reflected in movies, TV and novels. The series, "Sex in the City," dramatically portrayed how four women who cared for each other and supported each other through anything could so easily couple with men just because that's what one should do. They "fell in love," but there was always something wrong with the man, and he was soon dispensed with. Until the end of the series when magically each woman had found the right one.

Falling in love relieves the experience of shame for a time because both people are smitten. If someone is madly in love with you, you must be lovable after all! Then, when feelings subside, and the relationship falls into the ordinary, one or both can feel unloved. When falling-in-love is over, shame returns. Couples come to my office angry and critical of each other for no longer loving the way they did in the beginning. It's my job to help them see what they were really after, and how healing themselves is more productive than trying to get the partner to become what they want.

Most falling-in-love is not based on real caring, of truly adding to life. Those with toxic shame have difficulty engaging in such a pure manner. I want to jump up and shout to everyone, it won't work! Don't think it will work! Please, stay with yourself, learn how to heal shame, see how you medicate it, know that real love doesn't medicate it.

29. Impersonal Sex

One outcome of internalizing shame and defending against it is difficulty experiencing love and intimacy. If we are making ourselves up, hiding who we think we are, while yearning to be cared for, we will have difficulty communicating accurately. We will also have a hard time receiving real communication from others. When two people are together trying to talk, they will sense how little present the other person is. As the distance increases, they will try to create methods to feel close. Sex, even with strangers, is often used for that purpose.

Even less personal than sex with strangers is sex with pornographic images and fantasy. We know that much discomfort with sex can come from sexual abuse in childhood. Adult sex might trigger the emotions occurring back then. Impersonal, addictive, trance-based sexual acts can avoid those old emotions. And they can avoid the shame that was created by those abuses.

30. Being in a Relationship

According to the culture's rules single people are not living the right life, and are expected to feel shame. This forces many to get married. The rule has to be broken before it's possible to live alone and then discover what surfaces to be healed. It is possible to not need a relationship so that having one is only an addition to a good life.

31. Having Children

Coupling and having children is the right way to live, according to our genetic, community-creature instincts. It makes sense that two people bond tightly with sexual energy in time for the arrival of the babies that sex brings. Two people dividing the labor increase chances of survival. Of the many birds that bond for life, the ones I've observed work together to feed the babies. The albatross on Kauai are a lovely example of how the parents trade off sitting on the egg and tending the chick while the other parent goes diving for food.

In Southern California, quail walk along in a line. The chicks number over fifteen when tiny and silent, with about half remaining when reaching adult size. The full grown chicks need caretaking for a period, and they walk along with the parents who speak quietly.

Shame-based people have babies for less optimal reasons. Some women want someone who will always love them, have something to do, get or keep a man, or have an object on which to project their hatred and shame. Babies carry the shame of being used, unloved, and overtly shamed. They believe it is about them, not the parent.

32. Rote Living

Many habitual acts are valuable for leading an orderly life, such as showering and brushing teeth, eating breakfast, and countless other automatic acts that don't require thought. At the same time, all of us develop habits that actually interfere with spontaneous choice.

I admired my mother-in-law's sweater, and she said she liked it, too. She added that she wished she had a better figure under the sweater, more up here and less down there, but you can't have it all. She wasn't really feeling badly about this, she was following a long practiced habit. Later she looked at my computer, and when I said I was having trouble getting my email, she said, oh, you will! Both of these responses are not based on what is going on, they are stereotypical reactions to a situation or an emotion.

Many spouses depend on spending evenings with each other, and have difficulty when one starts spending time away from home. Sensibly, the at-home spouse should have a life of his own so that he carries it on even when his partner is gone. Single people figure this out with no problem.

Discussion in shame-healing groups can center on each person's exploration of habits that serve life and those that try to make life feel meaningful.

33. Becoming Disciplined

Discipline is necessary in order to work against obstacles that shame creates. If we had access to our full experience of life, we wouldn't need it. I have been told I have discipline, but I don't operate from any kind of motivator that feels like discipline. I follow my Feet. They take me in directions that lead me closer to being shame-free, and able to love as fully as possible. As my shame drops, my ability to love grows. Then I automatically operate differently. I don't try to love. I don't decide to love. I don't set goals. I don't have values to live up to.

Chapter 7: Early Shaming: Attachment Deprivation

Childhood deprivation of emotional attachment causes internalized shame.

We need to feel securely attached to our primary caregiver to feel safe and to believe that life is worth living. When children form a secure attachment in the first year of life, they know they are loved. Their needs are met with pleasure. The babies' instincts tell them this is right, and they have an appropriate experience of life - safe, secure, belonging, fitting in, having one's love received, being seen accurately, being understood. When the instinctive knowing of what is needed is satisfied, no shame is created. The child doesn't have to make up that something is wrong with him that has caused his mother to not do what is needed.

The securely attached child will grow up with shame, too, but it is shaming that comes later, and is moderated by the good first experience.

Lisa's mother became pregnant accidentally, and hid her pregnancy. Sylvia wasn't married and, with a career, the last thing she wanted was a baby. Lisa was clearly not wanted. More than not wanted, her mother had tried to abort her early in the pregnancy.

Lisa went to live with her mother and grandmother. The grandmother, retired and widowed, took over her care, as it provided her with something to do. Depressed, she lacked the ability to form a secure bond with a baby. Lisa wasn't loved in the way babies need.

What did this do to her? Lisa did what we all do. Seen as a bother and an inconvenience, she believed that the attitudes toward her reflected who she was. On a subconscious, non-verbal and elementary way she believed she was an abuser of her mother and a pet to her grandmother. Since she wasn't seen as the loving, curious, life-filled person she really was, she had to believe that their attitudes were accurate. She had no reflection of her real self.

One might say, yes, yes, that's too bad, but she did grow up and get a better life, didn't she? Well, she did create a better life, but she believed that she had little inherent worth to herself or anyone else.

Lisa internalized shame. The views of herself as bad were the foundation of her perception of herself. Then cultural shaming and all the unique forms doled out by parents and schools add onto this under layer.

Attachment deprivation causes the
deepest, most fundamentally
devastating shame.

Attachment in Infancy

A secure attachment in infancy and early childhood provides strength to defend against later shaming. Our experience of very early life has a powerful effect on our evolving attitudes toward ourselves. Any child who does not have a secure attachment grows up experiencing shame.

Children who receive little or no loving bonding will even die. Evidence comes from the study of babies in European orphanages during World War II who died in large numbers even while their needs for food, clothing, bathing, and diapering were being met. When it was understood that they needed to be held and loved and played with, volunteers were found. The babies stopped dying! They needed some sort of attachment, even if inadequate, in order to just stay alive.

Imagine what it would be like to have everyone around you project that you were unlovable, and unloving, and had nothing to offer. That you deserved nothing more than basic necessities. What would you think about yourself?

When this shaming is internalized the pain stays put. Self-criticism becomes part of your identity, part of the way you define your very being. Instead of a healthy view of oneself as lovable and loving, and growing up to discover gifts and interests, the attachment-deprived baby sees himself the way he is seen.

Lisa's mother was miserable, her grandmother depressed, and a baby wasn't welcomed. But Lisa, as the baby, couldn't understand that she had been born into a defective environment. Lisa's mother wasn't equipped to love a baby, particularly when she blamed the baby for what she had gone through.

When the child of disturbed, distracted parents looks to them for love he is going to believe that he is wrong, not wanted, outside, unloved, unlovable and unloving because the parent is unable to attend to him. Shame comes from how attachment figures relate, not just from overt shaming.

Believing one is unlovable
is a sign of internalized shame.

Some mothers don't know what children need, and who they are. They may fall back on imitating how other mothers act, or following rules for being a good parent. They may read books to "learn" about parenting, cut off from their inborn knowing of what is right for a child.

Children have no one to explain the parents' issues. We can learn the truth as adults, and then enter the grieving process to leave that view of self in the past. We can heal from the shame resulting from attachment deprivation.

Attachment Styles

Attachment theory has named four basic styles of attachment: secure, anxious, avoidant, and ambivalent. All of us experience a combination. We may have one dominant attachment style from which we operate most of the time, and another form that operates in certain relationships or situations.

Secure Attachment

Children automatically form a secure bond to the primary caregiver when she or he is emotionally available to the child. Research described in *Becoming Attached: First Relationships and How They Shape Our Capacity to Love*, by Robert Karin, demonstrated how these children feel safer when exposed to new situations. They have less stranger anxiety and can more freely engage in developmental tasks.

Lisa had no attachment with her mother, and only the constant presence of her grandmother. She had physical security, her needs for food and clothing and warmth were met. But her need for attention and a reflection of who she was didn't happen. Her grandmother felt put upon and resentful for having to care for a baby when she felt old, and struggled with depression.

Anxious Attachment

A child whose mother gives love and meets his needs, but is inconsistent, or from whom the child is separated for a time, may develop an anxious attachment. This is the clingy, needy child who often has difficulty starting school or staying with sitters. She feels shamed by the mother's depriving treatment, and then may be shamed for the resulting insecure behavior. The very expression of an anxious attachment brings even more shame!

As adults these people may become overly dependent on a spouse and over-value the experience of falling in love. A threat to the bond with the partner triggers the early childhood memory of being dependent on the parent for survival.

Lisa formed an anxious attachment to her grandmother and her mother even though neither were able to attach with her.

Avoidant Attachment

As I have said, this is the attachment style that I spent most of my live living, and have healed most of it away.

Babies who are inundated with attention that isn't based on their needs, or who are controlled to fit the parent's definition of successful parenting, or defined as bad or unwanted, may elect to avoid attachment rather than give in to an incorrect definition of themselves. Instead of clinging for physical survival, they pull away for the survival of their unique selves.

These are the babies who push away when held on a lap, who play quietly by themselves for a long time, who may just listen to their mothers from a distance.

An avoidant child must withdraw from the family in order to maintain a sense of self and not abandon herself. She elects to maintain her own gifts and offerings at the expense of giving up the shreds of love that are available.

As adults, avoidant attachers may be loners, preferring to limit time with others. They may be leaders or CEO's, in positions of power or control that put them at a distance from people. This separation can cause an intense need for a loved one, but comes with difficulty being with that person. A man may seek a mate for the bond that wasn't possible with his mother, but then pulls away as intensely as he sought it.

Avoiders try to avoid internalizing shame, but fail. I grasped onto avoidant attachment to prevent taking on the definition of myself as evil. It didn't avoid all shame, though. Shame is associated with the very need to pull away from other humans. The child wonders what is wrong with him that he can't fit in and belong.

If Lisa had only her grandmother's tolerant caretaking, she may have developed anxious attachment. But her mother's condemnation forced her to pull away from relating in order to maintain a sense of her right to be alive. Lisa developed anxious and avoidant attachments at the same time.

Attachment theory helped make sense of my childhood, as well as my adult ways of handling the memory of it. Avoidant attachment was the only reasonable approach to that childhood, even if it meant isolation in a family of five. When a child is defined as evil and harmful, one reasonable approach is to avoid attachment in order to not believe the definition. Though I was depressed as a child, and fell back into it when my son was born, it would have been worse if I had accepted my mother's definition of me.

What would I have done if I saw myself through her eyes? I could have had no conscience, and thought nothing of manipulating others to get what I wanted. Why would I hesitate? I would have lost my humanness if I accepted the definition of myself as evil.

Healing avoidant attachment has been unnerving because it had kept me human. I retained a sense of the rightness of life. My Feet were the source of understanding how it was right to live. Somewhere in the twisted thinking that arises out of crazy definitions of ourselves came the belief that I couldn't ever give up avoidant attachment. After all, it saved me from a horrible existence, or perhaps even death - like the orphans.

I've studied the countless small ways avoidant attachment influences relating. Our habits have to be examined for their original purpose, and by seeing them, we can let them go.

Ambivalent Attachment

Some children switch back and forth between anxious and avoidant forms of attachment depending on what is going on, and who they are with, as Lisa did. The adult form is the person who is frightened of losing a lover when the lover creates distance, but feels overwhelmed when the lover wants closeness.

Trying to Address Attachment Deprivation

One of my sexually addicted clients had been a sick baby, and was separated from his mother. Babies and young children can have a difficult time re-engaging in the bond that was present before separation. My client's addiction is focused on getting attention, saving others, and not being forgotten. He had interpreted his mother's abandonment to mean that he had been forgotten. He was deprived of really needed attention. He made up the belief that if he had been able to save others, he could have been valuable enough to be kept.

How the infant mind makes up these things is difficult for the adult intellect to understand. However, for the purpose of healing it is useful to accept that this is what a baby does.

The initial trust my client had that his mother wouldn't leave him was damaged when he was sent to the hospital. From then on he searched for a way of relating in which he will never be forgotten.

John Bowlby, the father of attachment theory, explains how children can't complete the grief process because their instincts tell them that if they let go of the parent (or a present-day stand-in), they will die. Back in hunting and gathering days, this was true. If the mother wandered off and forgot the baby, he would, of course, die. He needs to have his mother as attached to him as he is to her. The baby will express the anger component of grief in order to call out to the mother or her replacement. If no one comes forward, if he is truly abandoned, then he can complete the sad, letting-go emotion of grief, and die.

My client was trying, with adult behavior, to make infant sense of why he had been left. Perhaps if he thought his mother was dead, or the abandonment was irreversible, he would have died. By thinking it had something to do with what he had done, he could nurture hope of being different so that she would return. We can't know for sure, given his memory of that age, but we can make guesses that when they resonate with his emotions allow him to heal. He needs to cry. Now it is safe.

This man feels deep shame. More than the fear of dying from the loss of the maternal bond, he grew up with negative feelings about his face and body and people's interest in him. This is in spite of the fact that he is an attractive well-muscled athlete. He has friends, but doesn't develop relationships. In his social time he flirts with women to get attention. He can't obtain that intensity from friendship. Then he has to impress each woman with sex so she won't ever forget him. He masturbates to fantasies of women he has sexually pleased.

His intense attachment to sexuality suggests that he might have been abused. Research has shown that most sex addicts were sexually abused. However, the severity of his experience of abandonment alone can account for the use of sexuality to recreate the intensity of the needed childhood attachment. He experiences it as life-saving.

He is grieving for not having had constant attachment. Grieving for babyhood loss is long and deep - and possible. First he has to understand what happened. Then he has to give himself permission to grieve for what he can no longer remember. And he gets to perceive how he stops feeling shame with sexual feelings, and tries to use sex to recreate what he lost.

Attachment abuse causes internalized shame.

The culture thinks of abuse as physical, sexual and emotional, but the form of abuse that is interwoven with attachment can be severe. Attachment is the original need of infants, and remains with us through life as the need for community. Shunning is a harsh form of community punishment. We aren't intended to accept avoidant attachment as a way of life.

Parental shunning, known as the "silent treatment," is as devastating as beating. It is a silent statement on the child's lack of acceptability in the family. Trying to make sense of the pain, the child will accept the implication that he or she is not wanted, needed, or loved, and doesn't belong. Developing an avoidant attachment is one way to ward off the horror of this parental reaction.

Chapter 8. Shame From Harm We Caused

It is one thing to work on shame that we know shouldn't have been laid on us, but it is entirely different to look at the shame we feel because of what we did. The shame for what we have done or not done can feel excruciating. Shame for how we have harmed others. This is where we employ our most vigorous defenses against the feeling. You might find yourself saying things like, I did the best I could. I wanted to do it right, but couldn't help it when I couldn't. Or focus on things we did well.

Guilt is appropriate if we have caused harm. Toxic shame never is.

Those methods I described that we use to avoid feeling the internalized shame caused by others might be stepped up when looking at what we caused.

MADD (Mothers Against Drunk Drivers) began in Alaska when a severely intoxicated man ran down two children, killing them. How can he live with himself? Did he spend his life avoiding the shame? How did he avoid the shame of killing children?

A friend was dedicated to being a good mother, but her adult son is severely addicted and almost died of overdoses. How can she claim a full life for herself when she wasn't able to provide what he needed? The task of healing her shame is difficult. And possible. And appropriate.

I understand that my avoidant style was necessary to help me live as a child, and I have compassion for what I missed out on. It is another thing to think about harm I caused because of believing I had to stay removed from others.

I had a child in my twenties. I had become pregnant deliberately, intuitively understanding that having children is a correct experience. I went into post partum depression and began therapy when he was three weeks old. We had just moved away so my usual supports were no longer easily available.

My maternal instincts kicked in and I had severe reactions to the responsibility of motherhood. So while my son had a mother dedicated to giving the best care, he also had a mother who managed life through the lens of avoidant attachment.

Children are influenced by mothers who routinely experience painful emotions. Even while being committed to taking care of a child, we are limited by the focus on ourselves. We can't be fully present to the needs of the child. It is tragic that we can't decide to change that. We can't turn off the feelings, replacing them with what the child needs.

I had planned to go back to work, but quickly discovered that I couldn't leave him with others. Working had been a way to relate, and now I was in a house in a new town with no friends. My husband was more severely avoidant than I was, so between us we had little available to a child.

Now I have to face that using long established ways of protecting myself I harmed my child. And as I relinquish my remaining avoidant style, I have to face the shame of what I caused.

My son wasn't abused. He wasn't neglected. But he was deprived.

We Want to be Good Parents

We're so excited when learning that a little one is on the way. Families join together to welcome the new person. Even families that are upset over how their adult children behave are happy to hold a sweet little baby.

Everyone worries over the lack of sleep, the nature of poops, any evidence of problems. It brings us together.

We forget about the teen years, the issues of junior high school and high school. Grades, homework. We don't remember that these children will be broken too, along with all of us.

I was going to do it differently. I studied mothers, seeing how I would be with my child when he finally came. I was going to be better than other mothers.

I didn't know that my issues of avoidance would prevent me from being anywhere near the ideal.

Finding Our True Selves

How do we recover our true selves when we have harmed? We can begin with understanding that this is part of the human condition. We don't get to remain with the innocence we were born with. We received shaming, and internalized the beliefs that we are defective in one way or another.

Every single one of us has failed to be a perfect parent. Every single one of us has failed to be a perfect human being.

In order to find our true selves,
we must accept
our goodness and our badness.

If we feel toxic shame for our failings we cannot correct them because we can't look at them. We will use our long used ways of avoiding feeling shame, and this will also inhibit the correction of what we do that brings on that dreadful emotion.

Grieving for what we didn't do, or what we did that was harmful, can free us of the real guilt and real shame.

But first let's see if I can help you remove some of the shame.

Reducing Shame

I want to offer all of us an understanding of reasons we caused harm so that we can externalize some of our shame. If we go by the culture's view that we are all capable of being good people, of having high integrity, of doing everything based on a carefully made decision, then we should very well feel shame for failing.

But absolutely none of us fits that definition. Recent examples are the minister who wrote a book selling millions of copies who has shame about making millions of dollars doing something he enjoyed. He tells an interviewer that he lives in the same house, drives the same car, and gives the money to charitable projects. He started a church and has helped millions of people. Yet he can't pay off his shame.

Another person high in the church had road rage with several congregants in his car. This in spite of being seen as a caring, compassionate wise leader. He was both.

Even those who are revered and followed by many struggle with their lack of perfection, and with the accompanying shame. And yet if these people were perfect they would have difficulty understanding the needs of their followers.

Next is the shame that has been placed onto each of us, and how we all have our way of avoiding feeling it. Our avoidance prevents us from fully perceiving our children, and thus not being able to be entirely there for them.

Then comes shame integrated into the culture. We defend against it with denial, and then our own shame-avoiding methods. Being in community sets us up to figure out how to deal with our shame. And as we develop methods to avoid feeling it, we lose a little more of our ability to see the needs of children and other humans.

A cause of a person's distress that isn't heard of much is the experience that is carried down over generations. When our parents and grandparents didn't heal from their trauma and shame it is passed down to us. An understanding of this came when the children of holocaust survivors went to therapy with symptoms of being holocaust survivors. Their parents had to avoid their history, or talk about it from a victim stance. Their traumas were so horrendous they didn't have the strength to process and heal from it. Somehow it gets passed on to the next generation.

All four grandparents of a client survived labor camps when the war ended. He learned that the third generation carries the survivor's trauma emotions too. We traced some of his fears and dreams to the experience of his grandparents.

Each of us takes on some of the trauma and shame of past generations which can't be seen unless we engage in deep therapy. Even though you may not know what you passed on, you can know that not all of your ways of connecting are all about you.

What Did You Do?

I have focused on being with children since this dominates people's need to be responsible. It's wired into our instincts. As we know, sexual violation of children is considered by many to be more heinous than murder. There are countless actions that bring guilt and shame. However, toxic shame will not help us. It forces a disconnection from others. Real guilt can be used as a signal that something needs to change. Then you can change to relieve it. But toxic shame may prevent you from talking about it, seeing what you do, and making amends.

Lying

Lying is condemned, yet all people deceive to some extent. White lies, omissions, and exaggerations of accomplishments and other ways are used to try to make interaction flow more smoothly.

However, lying when having an affair, gambling, drinking secretly, or falsely reassuring a partner so they will stop being mad, is guaranteed to reduce your ability to perceive the real needs of others.

My one experience of ongoing lying was in high school when I dated someone my parents wouldn't have approved of. I lied about where I was and who I was with. I discovered that I could step into an acting role and play the part. I would look right at her and explain that I would be going to Karen's house after school, and her father would bring me home.

As an avoider I hadn't needed to develop the skills of deception because I lived on the outside of the family. None of us talked about personal things. But once I wanted to have an independent life I began lying. However, it was so painful that once away at college I knew I would never do it again. After going away to college I would withhold information about what I did, but I no longer stepped into the part and played it out.

When people have been betrayed by partners they most often say that being lied to is worse than the betrayal. When the couple work on reconciliation rebuilding trust is foremost. If toxic shame weren't felt by both, this would be a simple process. The betrayer could admit with guilt what he had done, and the lying. The partner could express devastation, but not feel as if she caused it or deserved it.

However, what usually happens is that their methods to not feel shame inhibit healing. She shames him for what he did which serves her desire to not feel shame for having a partner who would do this. By shaming him she doesn't feel her own.

He knows that what he did violated his integrity, and so could discover, for himself, how he can return to integrity. But if he has toxic shame he will give fake apologies, explain why it's her fault, or in some way justify what he did. Her toxic shame will react, and they will get into circular arguments.

Do you lie? How does it feel? How might you stop? Telling someone you trust could be a start as you figure out how to change. If the lies are compounded, it might feel threatening to begin revealing them.

Hurting People

Hurting others is usually at the top of the list of what people feel shame about. Those who hit partners feel terrible about it after the anger has subsided. The exception is psychopaths who have no conscience, but those are rare. Narcissists may seem to have no remorse because they are skilled at turning it on their victim. It's their fault, if they hadn't, I wouldn't have had to, etc. They do this in order to not feel their shame.

Here are some of the ways people hurt others. See what applies to you, and notice how you feel.

Shaming others. Criticizing, putting down, condescension, acting superior, naming his or her bad qualities.

Physically hurting. Hitting, pushing, grabbing, pinching, unwanted tickling.

Hurting people emotionally. Threaten abandonment, describe their flaws, say they aren't lovable, and so on.

Shunning, stonewalling. Becoming silent and withdrawn during a fight or argument, or because you believe the other person needs to be put in their place.

Passive aggression. Doing hurtful things that can be rationalized as not hurtful.

Being overly angry with rebellious children.

Subtle Harms

I have named ways we hurt others that aren't difficult to see. We carry shame for those things we can't see, too. I did not abuse or neglect my son, but he had a mother who lived with an avoidant attachment lifestyle, which deprived him. During his early years I did attach, and the strong emotions and responsibility were intense and disturbing. While he had a mother who attached during those early years, he also had a mother who was depressed and emotionally disturbed. Anxious. I projected my own childhood fears onto my concern for him.

The style I created to make myself safe from being harmed by my mother harmed my little child. As I had feared for myself, I projected danger onto him. Now I had to protect him, as I had had to protect myself.

I didn't learn the phrase avoidant attachment until I was in in my 30's, and it took many more years to understand that it described me. So I didn't know that not hitting or shaming or depriving wasn't enough. Looking back, I grieve for what I didn't get to experience. And foremost, of course, is how I deprived him.

Hitler, Etcetera

We are all good people and we are all bad people. When we try to be good, we are avoiding the very fact that we carry negative feeling toward ourselves. When we feel like bad people we are believing the shame voices in our heads.

Do we deserve to take care of ourselves and have good lives? This question reflects our belief in our badness, too. It is another way that we try to counter shame. If you work hard then you deserve. Or I deserve just because I am a person. These are attempts to deny shame that actually reinforces it.

We are living beings, made up of some particles and mostly energy waves, and that's all there is. We humans have made up that there is goodness and badness when really it is all about every single one of us carrying shame. You deserve more shame if you are bad, and you can reduce shame by being good.

Hitler and the Nazis believed they were doing something good by eradicating Jews. They didn't set out to be mean, they actually believed they were doing something good. Alice Miller studied Hitler's history and how he came to condemn Jews, explaining how his thinking directed him to get rid of the "bad ones." See *For Your Own Good: Hidden Cruelty in Child-Rearing and the Roots of Violence*. Miller demonstrates the ways children are harmed that are entirely congruent with the culture. They are unseen.

His reaction to his shame stands out because we see it as extreme. Killing six million people is horrific. But as long as we judge him as bad and ourselves as good we will continue to be influenced by our own shame. The truth is that we and Hitler have internalized shame. His way of avoiding it was extremely harmful, ours is less harmful.

What do you do so that you will be considered a good person? Do you lie, deceive, do things you don't really want to in order to be seen as good? Heart of gold, give the shirt off his back, always there for me.

Perceiving all of us as broken, and harmful, and helpful, can come from addressing our shame.

It's like the athletes who throw the highest number of passes or the most home runs or the winning touchdown. Or those with PhD and MD degrees, or the largest house, or the most money. When reaching the top brings self-esteem (avoidance of shame) dropping to the bottom will be devastating (shaming).

Self-esteem. This is another goal designed to reduce shame. If you feel good about yourself you feel better. You are high on your own ladder. What would it be like to have no ladder?

In my Buddhist meditation center we were advised to meditate on the thought of wishing every living being freedom from pain and suffering. It feels quite wonderful to do it, opens awareness of having that wish for everyone, for those living in integrity and for rapists and murders. Removing our own shame, our own hatred toward ourselves, will allow us to integrate this perception of humans.

Boundaries

It will be easier to establish boundaries, because of course you don't want others to walk on you just because you can see that they are neither good nor bad. From this rich place of perceiving all of humanity you can easily say no, or what you want or need. It won't matter if others shame you or think you are being unfair or inappropriate. It also won't change you when you are told how brave or smart or accomplished you are. You get to expand into life, safe from the whole subject of shame.

Chapter 9: Three Stories

In order to exemplify everyday shame that impacts all arenas of our lives and our communities, I am going to narrate the stories of three fictitious people. The first, Jack, grew up in a normal, loving family and received the normalized version of shame. Jack is one of those men who say they had a wonderful childhood, their parents did nothing wrong. Childhood can't have caused adult distress. When such men become my clients I walk them back through normal shaming that needs to be healed. They are usually upset when finding fault with parents who love them. Therapy groups can repeatedly establish that, while their parents really did love them, they passed on shaming from centuries of generations before them.

The second is Diana. She had even less shaming in her first two years than Jack, but sexual abuse added shame of greater impact.

The third is Maria, who began life with little attachment, followed by sexual and emotional abuse. She added self shaming with addiction and an inability to manage life well. While Maria doesn't seem to qualify as the recipient of acculturated, everyday shaming, she does. All those around her kept denying that she was being harmed. This fits into most of our cultural expectations because her parents looked good to the community.

These three people are fictitious, although their stories are accurate reflections of actual clients. This is in contrast to the other examples which are of real people but with identifying information changed.

Jack

Jack's parents wanted a child. Married two years, and in their late 20's, they were ready for a family and able to conceive. As the first grandchild on both sides, Jack was welcomed by extended family.

When he cried for "no reason" during the night, his mother worried that her husband would be upset. He had to have enough sleep to do well at work. They weren't surrounded by family as parents in the hunting and gathering days where help was always available. Jack's mother tried to get Jack to stop crying by anxiously rocking and bouncing him. She didn't like it when he wouldn't stop. She angrily whispered that he was a bad boy, didn't he understand that his father didn't like the noise? That he had to get his sleep?

His mother knew that Jack wouldn't understand her words, and her behaviors were well within the norms of our culture. But Jack picked up her tone and body tension, and received an energetic understanding that something was wrong with him. His only view of life was what his parents reflected, and so he believed on a deeply primitive level that something had to be wrong with him. This was his introduction to shame.

Jack had an advantage over children whose parents are unable to form a secure attachment with them. He could attach and feel safe and loved.

Occasionally, Jack's mother left him with one of his grandparents so she could sleep during the day. When she dropped him off, she shook her head and frowned, saying what a difficult child he was, and how good it was to be away from him for a few hours. Jack took in her tone, body tension, and energetic communication. He was too much work, he was a bother. He took on the shame of believing he caused unhappiness.

There were many happy times, too, such as playing patty cake and laughing so hard playing peek-a-boo. He felt wonderful and safe and loved when he was nursing, and when his dad snuggled him up, making soft, cooing noises. They went on picnics, and both parents played with him, smiling and happy.

After Jack learned to crawl, he got into things. His mother swatted him and firmly said, "No!" He used these times to begin monitoring his behavior. But when she shook her head, frowning, and looking distraught, he felt somehow not right. This was different from learning rules to follow, or breaking them and hearing "no." She seemed to want to get rid of him, to relegate him to his room and leave him alone. She didn't like being around him. His shame grew.

When Jack was two, and his mother dressed him up for a family gathering, he ran outside and fell onto muddy ground, then fondled the wet soil. The family was late, and both parents scolded him angrily while changing his clothes. He understood that he should have known. He felt shame for who he was - someone who didn't know. He couldn't understand what they wanted those many times they treated him like a bad boy, a child who wanted to cause problems. He hadn't played in the mud to make them unhappy. He liked mud.

The parents could not see what was going on inside their son's mind because they had been raised the same way they were raising him. They thought their scolding was not harmful, and their frustrations justified. They had grown up in our emotionally cut-off culture, and had lost their own deep sensitivity. They truly didn't know that their shaming frowns were registering, and adding up year after year. Their lost sensitivity was passed onto their child, even though they were dedicated, loving parents.

All parents shame their children.

We can gather together in order to accept this as a fact. We don't need to shame ourselves for it.

When Jack was three and four, his mother was glad that she hadn't used the disciplinary methods her own mother had used. She didn't spank him, she didn't yell at him. She didn't say, "bad boy." She thought expressing annoyance was so much better. She didn't know that this conveyed shame, too. The tone implies that the recipient is just so stupid, so inconsiderate, so needing to be different, even if the words are neutral. She didn't know this. She was pleased that she didn't use overtly harmful methods.

Jack accumulated a little shame with each comment. His aunt and other adults gave no indication that his mother's tone was not appropriate, and so he had no mirror of the truth. Everyone was in agreement that the treatment was right. If he had heard only one adult tell his parents that they were shaming Jack, and they needed to learn to stop so he wouldn't take it in, he would have had an accurate mirror. This might have helped him know that his parents were wrong when they shamed him, and he might have taken in less. But the whole culture believes that these parents were appropriate in their discipline, and deserved sympathy for the difficult task of raising a young child.

Jack's parents valued education and taught him many things before he started kindergarten. He loved the attention, and so he worked hard to learn. He couldn't know that formal education was not the direction that would help him discover his gifts and talents. He loved to draw, and move things around to look different. Adults said, that's nice, but they didn't help him develop this fascination. They were unable to perceive that education was their interest, not his. They didn't see that he had his own interests. This is not because they were selfish, narcissistic people; it was because they were typical products of living in our culture. Their own shame-based understanding of humanness had been short-circuited by shaming throughout their lives.

As they defended against the feeling of shame by accepting the cultural mores, they lost their ability to know everything about themselves and about their child.

After starting school, Jack was annoyed much of the time. He didn't know why, because no one was able to provide a reflection of his emotions. When he pouted and refused to do what he was asked, he was met with more shaming. His parents, so full of love and affection, had no idea why he would act this way. They had truly done nothing inconsistent with our culture's definition of good parenting.

Jack's annoyance and mild rebellion were his way of claiming his unique self, his developing personality. He couldn't communicate that he didn't like the shaming and control of his development. All he could do was try to refuse it.

When Jack was five, his parents took him on a road trip. Jack didn't like to sit quietly for long periods, and tended to complain. This time he set out to enjoy himself and not object. He told his parents about this, and he stopped himself each time he shifted into being negative. This pleased them, and they told him how good he was - he was a good boy.

This evaluation shamed him, too, because it carried the implication that if he stopped, he would be a bad boy. Instead of being told he was good, he needed smiles and support for determining his own task, and the pleasure it brought him when succeeding. This would affirm him. "Jack, that was so cool how you set out to act in the way you wanted, and you did it!" This is different from telling him that he had successfully done what they wanted.

Even while Jack's parents shamed him many times every day, they also tried to help him not feel shame! Our culture has countless methods to relieve people from this very emotion that it creates.

Jack's parents told him not to worry about getting only a B in math, they knew he was smart. They explained that he would grow into his long legs. They said, "Oh, don't feel bad, honey," when his friends had a gathering and didn't invite him. If we had no acculturated shame, he wouldn't have valued these de-shaming statements. They would have had no value because he would have had no shame.

By the time Jack was in the first grade he knew how important performance was to his parents, and he set out to get good grades. He succeeded, and they exclaimed over each report card. Again, good parenting according to the culture. But when the child learns what to do to be rewarded, he is distracted from following his intuition and interest in developing himself. Lucky are the children where the reward matches the child's interests. My family valued education for its own sake, and luckily, education was needed to create the right career and life for who I am. However they didn't support my education for this reason.

When children conceal their intuition, preferences, emotions, gifts, and personality in order to please parents, they lose sight of themselves. They will stop knowing what they want through the psychological defense mechanisms of repression or denial. Anger and tears, those vital emotions of grief that are needed to leave the past in the past, are blunted, withheld, ignored and shamed.

Even when children are trained to tell parents or other adults if inappropriately touched, they usually don't. When a relative or family friend is sexual with a child, the child will feel shame for having received this kind of attention, and will want to hide it. Their sexuality has already been laden with acculturated shame, and the subject so avoided for discussion, that the child can't separate typical acculturated sexual shame from the shaming from behaviors done to them.

Even though he had not been physically or sexually abused, Jack was angry. He didn't know why. His outbursts and hitting other children were, of course, shamed. This increased the amount of shame he internalized. The school counselor leaned forward, looked him in the eyes, and seriously asked why he hit the other child. Neither she nor Jack understood that there was no present-day answer.

In addition to receiving the rules for goodness from his parents and the school, Jack was taken to Sunday school. There he was taught the Ten Commandments and other rules. He learned that being good was the right way to be. If Jack had not been shamed, he might have discovered that the rules actually agreed with his understanding of how humans get along best. Instead of rules, he would have had reflections of what he knew deep inside. But for a child with layers of shame internalized into his identity, religion became one more source of shame for making him feel that he didn't fit in with the culture's definition of goodness.

Religion gave him a method of feeling good about himself, too, in spite of his growing sense of badness. By following the rules he could be seen by others as good. Amazing. However, he retained a sense that something was incorrect. But this was better than nothing, better than feeling different from others. Jack became a "good boy."

Along with all children, Jack discovered that he could inhibit shame by doing certain things. His parents had modeled rationalizing. It wasn't my fault, I didn't mean to. But this didn't go very far in getting rid of this horrible emotion. Over time he learned that if he shamed other people, he would stop feeling it himself. He started with his sister, and when she melted into a crying puddle, he felt powerful. He didn't like to hurt her, but his need to get rid of shame was strong enough to make it worthwhile. Then he repressed his guilt by believing that she deserved it, and that she was too weak to take it.

Next, he shamed his friends. Soon he discovered that some friends liked to shame others, too, and they aligned with each other. Four boys became bullies, laughing at how easy it was to humiliate people. They even shamed their parents. They watched to see what made them feel bad, and then went after it. Jack made his mother feel like a bad mother, and his father a failure in his career, even though he wasn't. He held up high standards, then criticized them for not measuring up. With sarcasm he said, "Dad, now tell me, why didn't you get that promotion? Are you sure it wasn't that you just weren't good enough?" To his mother, "Mom, I know you try hard to cook, but what is this stuff?" Both parents began hating him, but couldn't let themselves know it. They knew it was wrong for their son to speak to them like this, and they had no idea why he did.

Jack diminished his guilt by rationalizing that his parents were inadequate human beings who needed to be spoken to this way. However, he couldn't override his need to please his dad by going to college and majoring in engineering.

By the time Jack reached puberty, his sexuality had been shamed, even though his parents tried to be accepting. From infant erections, to the age three delight in his penis, to the age four sexualized longing for his mother, to the sexual shame projected from all those adults who were feeling their own, he felt shame the first time he masturbated. Normal childrearing in this culture creates sexual shame in everyone. Instead of being amazed by the strong sexual feelings, the erection and the ejaculation, he was mortified. He immediately knew that this powerful experience had to be kept secret. His male instinct to perpetuate the species prevented him from giving up sexuality in order to avoid the shame. So he continued to masturbate, even though each time more sexual shame was layered over the last.

On some deep, unconscious level, Jack resented having to hide his sexuality. So he showed off around his peers. They joined together by joking and looking at girls' body parts and making lewd comments. This acculturated male behavior angrily pushes back the shaming! He'd show them how he wasn't going to give in to feeling bad, he'd do what they didn't like and there was nothing they could do about it! He felt powerful and shame-free. But each time a little more shame had been layered on. This pushed him to again be boldly rude and obnoxious to turn off the dreadful emotion.

Jack's innocent, loving parents had no idea why their son acted like this. They ascribed it to his age, saying teens are like this, he will outgrow it. If they had taken

Jack to a counselor, the counselor might very well have agreed, and assisted the family in handling present-day conflicts. Things might have gotten better, but the internalized shame would not be addressed. Parents can't understand that their children are reacting to normal parental behaviors. They don't know that their actions are harmful.

Jack knew on some level that he was seeking integrity by being angry and rebellious. He was punishing his parents for hurting him, which was pointless and didn't change anything. But if he had apologized, he would have felt more shame, as he would have taken on responsibility for the family problems. Either way, his shame would multiply.

The lack of understanding of how adults shame children from birth, and in every facet of their lives, leaves all families unable to understand their children's problematic behavior, and unable to find solutions.

Jack did well in school in order to make his parents happy and proud. He had a series of relationships, but as each woman sought to change him in some way, he became angry. Over time he found fault until either she or he ended it. He thought all women must be bitches, and thought he might not marry.

Again, his parents couldn't make sense of this because they had modeled a good, solid marriage, and thought he would follow suit. It made no sense to Jack or anyone around him that he was combating shame. He tried to avoid feeling it by staying away from shamers, or by being really good, or by shaming and attacking others. He didn't have to feel it when he won in a competition or got all A's or got drunk with the guys. He achieved relief from this dreadful controller of life. Of course he had to cut himself off from a good deal of his humanness in order to not feel shameful, but it was worth it.

He didn't yet know that he could feel the shame, let it move through him, and discharge it. He could heal it. He could reclaim his humanity.

When turning thirty, Jack fell apart. He hated his engineering job and dreamed about following his interest in art. He was constantly angry, finding fault with everything. He joined a therapy group and gradually came to recognize the normal, acculturated shaming that had dominated his childhood. At last he heard a roomful of people agree that his childhood shaming had been harmful. Once he could grieve it out, he began to smile and laugh. He saw how he had accumulated shame, how he had internalized it, and how he had defended against experiencing it.

Because Jack had a secure childhood attachment with his mother, and was well loved by many, his progress was rapid. Adults who have been seriously abused take more time when relieving the various forms of shame and trauma. In a few months Jack could look at people around him and recognize when they were shaming each other. He could identify reactions to the shaming, the defensiveness, the circular arguments, how TV commercials showed women shaming men, "friendly" put-downs, gossip.

Next he was able to see what he did to not feel the shame, to defend against it. He could gradually stop, let the shame emerge, and discharge it. At last he could understand the role of the culture, and how his beloved parents had unknowingly passed it on.

Jack was able to tell his parents that he was going to art school, and that even if he wasn't financially successful with art, that was acceptable to him. A year later he started dating, and quickly saw which women would continue to shame him even after he told them not to. He found a woman who was interested in learning about cultural shaming so she could stop, too.

Diana

Sexual shame is a powerful force, as I have described. It inhibits the loving use of sex, and can distort the life of people who are otherwise not highly shamed.

Diana was forty-four when she entered a therapy group. Her children were grown, and she was trying to understand why her life felt somewhat empty. She woke with nightmares of being held down and not being able to breathe. She had never encountered anything like this before and couldn't make sense of it. Her physician prescribed anti-depressants, but she didn't want to take them. She wanted to understand what was happening to her, and what she might do about it.

Her therapist saw her individually for several months before recommending group therapy because she could see that Diana's shame about her sexual relating was too strong to be able to reveal it to others. As they examined the dreams and the body memories, it became clear that Diana had been sexually abused in early childhood. She was able to take the cloudy film off old memories, and realize that she had been molested by an uncle who had lived on and off with her family.

Diana's marriage had gone along smoothly by the standards of the culture. She and her husband had figured out how to solve problems, and both complained to friends about the other instead of engaging in painful circular arguments. Diana had sex with her husband because she believed this was required of her as a wife. But a few years earlier, when her distress began to mount, she could not bring herself to be sexual in any way.

Like Jack's, Diana's parents were loving and affectionate, and all three children were wanted. Both enjoyed the activities of children at different ages, and their lives were richly defined by family. They provided secure attachments and were able to see and support their children's interests and abilities.

Diana encountered shame later than Jack. Her mother, Fran, had a lot of help from sisters and her own mother. She was able to sleep when needed, which gave her an unusually good experience of new motherhood. Two sisters had children and could understand what she was going through. They listened well. Diana's father, Richard, was so happy to have a second child, a girl after a boy, that he was glad to go home right after work and be with both children. Neither parent was upset over dirty diapers or the baby's crying as they had been with their first. The second was so much easier compared with the shocking life changes the first brings. Their pleasure made it unpleasant for them to shame the baby, and also to shame each other! Diana got off to a good start.

When Diana was old enough to discover that touching her genitals felt good, and she lit up, both parents said nothing. They had read that the child should not be stopped or scolded. They didn't know that their discomfort over watching a child stimulate herself was transmitted anyway. Since all people carry sexual shame, whether they are aware of it or not, they cannot help transmitting it to their children. When I ask clients how their parents taught them about sex, almost everyone says that it wasn't talked about. Most of the parents who did talk about it did so in unhealthy ways. I almost don't believe it when someone describes a good history of communication about sexuality.

The only time most people can talk about sex is if engaging in it, or when integrating shame into the discussion: calling sex bad, dirty, nasty while poking the other in the ribs and laughing. Joking. Did you get some? I got lucky. And on and on.

Sex is not an ordinary subject in everyday conversation. It is rare to hear someone say something like, My husband and I had really nice sex last night. We were both relaxed, and it just unfolded naturally into a good bonding exchange. Orgasms aren't mentioned except in joking tones, or complaints about lack of.

Parents can believe that by saying nothing they are communicating nothing. But babies pick up energetic communication, and older children understand when something is out of bounds for discussion.

When Diana was three, her uncle came to live with the family in order to save on expenses while in college. He was a shy young man, so when he discovered that his niece was warm and loving, he appreciated it. He offered to baby-sit when the parents wanted to shop or go out to dinner.

Diana loved the attention of this man who lived with them, this member of her family. She snuggled with him while they watched TV, and followed him around when he worked in the yard or did his wash. She trusted him.

One day when she sat on his lap, he became aroused. At first he was shocked, but he had no lover and he missed contact like this. So he moved her body to increase his arousal, thinking she wouldn't know what he was doing. When she wanted to get down, he held on to her because he became focused on his arousal and not her needs. As she fell forward to get off his lap, he caught her by the neck, his focus now on his coming orgasm. He didn't know she was crying and fighting him.

Once he lost arousal after orgasm, he realized what he had done. He put her down and ran to his room where he changed his clothes. He was horrified. He became sullen and quiet.

Diana didn't like having her uncle treat her badly, but she could have bypassed that trauma because of her love for him. But having him withdraw from her and the family was devastating. She thought he stopped loving her. She was afraid he was leaving. So she sought him out, holding his hand and trying to get him to look at her.

The parents watched their brother turn away from the little girl, and they felt sorry for her. They talked with him about spending more time with her, asking what was wrong that he didn't like her anymore. He couldn't explain, and he couldn't change the feelings.

A week or so later, the parents were gone for a couple of hours, assuming it would be good to leave Diana with him. This time when she tried to touch him, she reached for his penis since this had been important to him. He became aroused, and again held her on his lap until he reached orgasm.

Diana was torn between getting attention, and losing him to his sexual trance. If this was the only way she could get attention, she might do it again. But she felt icky when he did that thing. And she felt badly about herself afterward. Her sexual shame, and his shame, and the way he disappeared from their real relationship were very upsetting. When her uncle moved out of the house two weeks later, she missed him terribly but was relieved. The struggle between wanting him and not wanting the sexualized relating was gone.

In nursery school that fall Diana shied away from men who came to get their children or who worked there. When her parents noticed this, they wondered what was going on in the school, and moved her to a different one. Over time, Diana reacted less and less.

When she became a teenager, she was puzzled over the contrast between wanting the attention of boys but not wanting to get close. Her sexual feelings brought her back to that long-ago experience. It was no longer a picture-memory, so she couldn't connect her teen experience with what happened when she was three. She didn't date until she was in college, and then she advanced slowly. At the same time, she yearned for physical contact with a man she liked. She wanted that sexual feeling and touch. But along with desire came shame.

She met Ted her second year of college and fell completely in love with him. She knew he was a perfect mate, and so she had to become sexual. At first she had several drinks before even kissing. She was terrified as clothing gradually came off. With weeks of working up to it, she calmed her fears with sexual arousal and committing to this man. She was not aware that sexual shame had become embedded into her being from the interactions with her uncle.

Ted felt the same way about Diana, and so was patient with her sexual issues. He knew it was more important to bond into a couple than to have good sex because she was a compatible mate. He wanted to marry her when they were out of school.

They had sex regularly. Diana set no limits as she knew she had issues that weren't his fault. She had orgasms, and experienced pleasure, but if Ted were on a business trip she was relieved to avoid sex. She didn't question this. It just seemed to be the way she was.

Children and her career occupied her, and she went to church to understand how it was right to live her life. She believed she was a good person and hadn't accumulated negative feelings about herself. Her general internalized shame was mild compared with the average person's, but her sexual shame was high. This was more or less avoided by seeing sex as something she needed to do and was all right to enjoy.

The emotions that emerged when she was forty-four were shocking. She knew she needed to do something about them. Her therapist specialized in sexuality and could quickly see that her issues had to do with sex. In asking about Diana's childhood, not just the sexual parts, the therapist was able to discover the presence of the uncle who went from being deeply loving to distancing himself. She understood why people do this and slowly elicited Diana's memory. Because Diana was three, she had no clear picture of the sensation of the erect penis against her, or the hand on her throat. She did have the body memory of both, because she couldn't tolerate having her neck touched, or sitting on a man's lap. Her therapist took her back to those discomforts several times, and each time Diana cried or raged against her uncle. In several months she was freed from the memories and could think of them without much emotion.

Next, her therapist worked toward touching her throat. First she extended her hand, and let Diana have the fear that emerged. Finally, Diana was able to allow her therapist to gently touch her throat. She cried with relief and amazement. A similar process with her husband resulted in being able to sit on his lap, and finally do so when he had an erection.

Diana's progress was rapid because her overall level of shame was low. Therapy could focus on sex. Usually when addressing sexual abuse, people have to address other sources of shame, and the devastating feelings caused by the parents' lack of protection. Diana did this, but it went quickly because she had had a secure attachment with both parents, her relationship with them as an adult was strong and loving, and she had a solid, loving relationship with her husband.

Diana was grateful to be relieved of the emerging emotion memory, and just as glad to discover a true interest in sex. What had been a duty became a pleasure. She felt as if she were falling in love with her husband again as she hadn't been able to use sexual energy and activity in her initial bond with him. A low-shame person himself, he could join her in this new experience of their marriage.

Julie

Julie's history is typical of what therapists encounter. Not only did her stepfather molest her, he blamed her for it by saying that she was too attractive and made him do it. He also shamed her for not being attractive enough. This man was too narcissistic to understand her feelings and needs. He wasn't capable of love and had no way to perceive what was going on. His own shame required high use of denial and alcohol. He couldn't afford to understand his stepdaughter's feelings because if he did, his shame would mount to unacceptable levels.

Julie's mother oriented her attention to her troublesome second husband, terrified that if she didn't take good enough care of him, he would leave, too. Her despair was so strong that she couldn't know what her daughter needed. If she had, she would have felt immense shame and would have had to take action to protect her. She turned away, basically giving her child to her husband to do with as he pleased.

Julie adopted a great amount of shame from sexual abuse, and she also took the lack of love and caring to mean she wasn't lovable or deserving. This was further compounded by criticism from both parents. They wanted to avoid their shame for how they parented. They used criticism as a powerful way to avoid their own shame. Instead they saw Julie as shame-worthy.

School was hard for Julie, so she felt stupid, furthering her shame. She wasn't able to pay attention in class or when reading because she daydreamed about the future. She used the psychological defense mechanism of dissociation to avoid pain. Dissociation can be emotional, intellectual, or physical, or all three. When intellectually dissociated, Julie couldn't learn facts. Her brain wouldn't allow it.

Reaching puberty and discovering strong sexual feelings, she was confused. These were the bad feelings, yet they felt good. As she developed, her stepfather laughed at her body, while her mother feared his attraction would be stronger for the girl than for herself. The already bad dynamics became worse.

Then magic happened. Boys started looking at Julie's body and became really interested in her. Attention of any kind felt good, and she was already accustomed to sexualized attention. She quickly learned how to flirt and dress in provocative ways. Power came from choosing one boy and making it clear to the rest that they didn't qualify. She began having intercourse when she was thirteen.

By the time Julie reached high school she discovered the price to be paid for using sex this way. She was placed in the slut category by other girls. They shamed her, adding one more layer. Being used for sex by boys had already compounded her stepfather's conveyance of shame.

Julie started drinking when fourteen, and added drugs as the years went on. She had to use more and more to keep the shame at bay. She wanted to avoid tremendous anxiety and depression that she sensed was right there waiting to grab her.

When a child becomes promiscuous, and drinks and uses drugs, people wonder what is wrong with her. Why does she have hangovers, why does she go out with many boys, why why why? In the last two decades it is better understood that sexual abuse can cause such symptoms. But to get help the child has to tell.

A twenty-eight-year old client was still apologizing to her parents for drinking and using drugs and not obeying their rules in her teen years. She felt bad for the trouble she caused them! She came to see me after she told her parents that her grandfather had molested her from the time she was seven until she was eleven years old. She couldn't tolerate being around him at family gatherings, and her life had been in upheaval.

Julie's stepfather was a professor of engineering at the local university. He was highly respected for his research and teaching ability. Her mother was a fifth grade teacher appreciated by her colleagues and parents. No one would have suspected what Julie was going through. Most didn't believe it when they learned. They took the parents' side.

Somehow Julie managed to get into a local college, but had difficulty going to classes because of staying out late and suffering hangovers. Finally, she felt so terrible that she seriously wanted to die. Deep shame for her behaviors along with feeling unlovable, unwanted, and merely something to use, were too much. She started saving anti-depressants that hadn't relieved her depression, and planned to consume them with a lot of alcohol.

While she was planning her death, her mother called. She had finally ended the marriage, and wanted Julie to come home for the weekend to take care of her. Julie felt a wash of rage, and screamed into the phone. She told her mother that she had never been taken care of, that her mother had stayed with this horrible man who abused her and did nothing about it, and that, no, she wasn't going to take care of a woman who had never been a mother!

She slammed down the phone and threw the medication out. Storming out of her room, she charged across the campus to the counseling center. With more energy than she had felt in a very long time, she demanded that the receptionist give her someone to talk to right then. She was escorted to an office, and poured out the story of her whole miserable life.

With the help of the counselor, she went to AA, and got support in giving up the chemical method of avoiding shame. She felt amazingly good as her body healed from the assault of alcohol. Her counselor warned her that the shame would emerge once she stopped using these ways of avoiding it. Sure enough it did. But nothing was worse than feeling suicidal. She responded well to support for righteous anger at both parents, even while this did not include expressing it directly. It was clear that they were both so disturbed they wouldn't be able to give her the response that she needed to assist healing.

The combination of shame beginning with being unloved, compounded by sexual abuse, then overlaid by ongoing harsh criticism, left Julie with a great deal of shame to challenge, discharge, and grieve out. She went to therapy for five years, and continued in a group and AA for much longer.

Chapter 10: Love and Community

Previous chapters address the facets of shame and their effects on individuals. What might community be like if toxic shaming were not integrated into everyday life? *The Continuum Concept*, by Liedloff, offers excellent information about a shame-free culture. The author describes a tribe in South America where she lived for a time. It offers a model of how we are intuitively guided to interact, and the life that is possible if we follow it. The level of toxic shame is low within the culture and for individuals.

In her novel, *The Kin of Ata Are Waiting for You*, Dorothy Bryant introduces a culture that beautifully integrates unique gifts and qualities into a fluidly working community. This shame-free functioning offers healing to a man who has all the worst characteristics of shame-driven people. He rapes, uses, discards, and eventually murders. We easily see how he struggles against the members of this community, but finally comes to understand. He heals his shame and develops his unique gifts.

Our Unique Selves Integrated into Community

When we are fully ourselves, fully boundaried, and vulnerable then we can join in community with others with no sacrifice, no controlling, no being controlled. Love and our innate positive understanding of how to work well together have a chance to emerge. The self is valued and supported, and communes with the self of everyone else.

Each unique person can merge into community with no loss of the self.

Liedloff describes how babies were held as long as they wanted while mothers went about their daily tasks. People laughed together as they completed difficult projects. No one acted like victims or abusers or rescuers. They didn't need to because they had not lost their ability to commune. One man returned after a long time in the city and enjoyed sitting around, taking advantage of everyone else's labor. He had lost touch with the natural understanding of his people. They talked to him with concern, hoping he would come to see that having a good life meant joining the community, doing his part, giving what was good for him to give. They were pleased for him when he came to this understanding, and began farming.

Each of us can heal shame in order to access natural instincts that members of this tribe followed. Solutions to our community problems would then naturally unfold.

Secure Attachment

A healthy, shame-free culture would provide secure attachments for all children. The child's needs would be met first by the primary caregiver, usually the mother. As he becomes social and then mobile, his attachment would expand to include the father and other adults.

People without shame can fully perceive this need. Few people have this to offer. They offer attachment on a continuum from good to none. This implies that if all parents were shame-free, and thus had access to intuitive understanding of the needs of humans at all ages, all children would be provided with a secure attachment! Liedloff's observations support this.

I have described attachment styles in past chapters. *Becoming Attached*, by Robert Karen gives the history of the theory and research and their current focus in psychotherapy. A simple understanding is in *Attached:*

The New Science of Adult Attachment and How It Can Help You Find - and Keep – Love, by Amir Levine.

The style of attachment formed by the child with its primary caregivers influences how he will relate with attachment figures in adult life, and how he might handle acculturated shaming. When children are offered the opportunity for secure attachment, they interpret that as meaning something about them. Born with instincts telling them what to expect from life, they will comfortably merge into the family, safely knowing their needs are met, and quickly exchange lots of love. Babies enter the community immediately.

Supported by a secure bond, the child has the freedom to travel along at the prescribed developmental pace, reaching each natural milestone in time. Rolling over, standing, tearing paper, walking, talking, running away from Mom and then quickly back to her, counting, and all the way through school into adult developmental tasks. The child's unique gifts and interests and abilities appear. He gets to place importance on his personal explorations and develop them along with the shared tasks. The needs of the community will flavor the development of his offerings.

If a person has received sufficient attention to his needs as an infant and in childhood, with parents who were able to perceive his communications, he will grow up feeling securely attached to them and others. This doesn't ensure emotional health, but it provides a valuable foundation.

The securely attached person is
capable of being well integrated
into the family and into the culture.

Outgrowing the Need for Attachment

Healthy attachment responds to the real needs of the child. At birth he is entirely dependent, trusting that his mother will be there for his every need. Love welcomes him into community. He instinctively uses angry crying to get her attention if she strays, bringing her awareness back to him. When he learns to walk, and can feed himself, his dependency diminishes.

By the time he is five he requires very little because he has bonded with many adults and peers. At nine he needs a home and meals and boundaries, as his attachment with friends grows. He has entered community. By adulthood, he has outgrown his need for attachment to his parents. He provides his own meals and shelter, and depends on all around him for love and communing. When ready, he couples with another person and creates his own family. His relationships with parents and siblings change. Parents become grandparents to his children. Eventually he will have responsibility to care for them. Affection and shared history and blood loyalty remain, along with membership in the larger community.

In our culture of social isolation, family has taken on too much meaning. It is difficult to outgrow that attachment because we cannot replace it with a solid community. Having a spouse and children is the closest we can come.

None of us had the security to allow us to outgrow attachment. Society prescribes putting the baby in his own bed and carrying him in a carrier. His parents shame prevents them from sufficiently accessing themselves in order to entirely access his needs. They are not capable. No one can have a truly secure attachment.

The adult who has grown out of childhood attachment will know what to do when his parents age and approach death. He will become responsible when it is appropriate. He will perceive their real needs and meet them. He won't do this because of the rules, or to feel like a good person, or even because he loves them. He will access innate knowing that this is what humans are to do. It is part of our inherent integrity.

Vital Connection

Love is a central quality of human life that brings us true awareness of being alive and in community. Love brings pleasurable responsibility for meeting the real needs of others, and satisfaction when we succeed. The pleasure of parenthood comes from taking on the needs of the baby as our own. Pleasure when meeting real needs is who we are as humans. We will do so unless shame or other obstacles prevent the satisfaction.

*Healing individual and cultural shame
allows us to become human*

We have all had experiences in which the pressure of shame was lifted, and we became able to access our humanness. Natural disasters connect people, providing a deep sense of togetherness and love. Earthquakes, fires, floods, and hurricanes bring us together. Nine eleven in particular united and connected us. We briefly got to experience the community that is our human heritage.

Singing or chanting together in large numbers, attending concerts, and even movies in theaters allow us to join with others for a while. Meditating in large groups brings an escalating energetic connection. We are taken out of ourselves more completely than when we watch TV because so many join in the experience.

The tragedy is that we don't get to commune all the time when involved with the simple tasks of life. Food, shelter, transportation, exchange of goods and services, and all the basic needs.

The night Barack Obama was elected to the presidency millions of us cried together, touched by this amazing event. The magnitude of it brought us together even though we were all over the world. The strength of the shared feeling stopped our shame! With shame out of the way, we became human!

But it couldn't last. Shame and blaming and divisiveness will prevail because individuals need that to stop the experience of shame.

Wars can create unity. The population bands together to fight a justified cause. When a war becomes unpopular, those on one side bond together against those on the other.

Working well together is the natural state of humans. We are designed to love, and accept love, and help each other, and create a well working order that supports the best in everyone. So why is this rare? Why do we depend on emergencies, weddings, illness, injury, natural disasters, and death of loved ones in order to feel communally engaged? Why can't we have this experience all the time? Why do we have to use intensity to override the obstacles?

The answer is: Internalized toxic shame permeates the culture.

Healthy Shame and Guilt

The healthy forms of shame and guilt are mild emotions that flow through us, alerting us to what we need to do to support love and cooperation and pleasure and meeting the real needs of others in the community.

Healthy shame is simply a soft, gentle pull forward toward serving ourselves, and in so doing, serving our community, our country, our world. The absence of war would be natural. Of course we wouldn't kill each other or rob each other's resources.

I went into a very crowded store to pick up my computer. I thought all I had to do was walk in and have it handed to me as I had already paid for it. The man who said he would help me helped two other people first. I interrupted him to say that all I wanted was to pick up my computer. He went to get it. Then I discovered that the process took ten minutes while he got the computer out, turned it on, and had me check it. I saw that of course I shouldn't have been served before others who were there before me. I told him I wanted to apologize for my attitude as I hadn't known it would take that time. I had no toxic shame. I could see that he was owed an apology or an explanation. I could right my implied criticism, which was out of order.

Regardless of how he responded, I felt good. I had returned to my well lubricated cells all working together. Period. The interesting thing is that I was pulled to do this, not pushed by shame. I felt better, cleaner, and in my integrity. I removed an obstacle to the pleasure of my day. I did it for me! And because I wasn't operating from toxic shame or asking to be forgiven, I could give him a gift of the two of us being together, working on this task. When I am in my integrity, I can care and give.

When shame is healthy,
it is not unpleasant.

Words like sacrifice, and meeting the child's needs instead of your own, are the result of being cut off from our humanness. With no shame, and knowing our integrity, we would need to meet the needs of our children. I needed to take care of my son. I didn't do it to be good, to follow rules, to do what's right. There was no sacrifice, no compromise. I did it because I needed to. This was even though parenting was frightening, demanding, and exhausting.

Being Alone or Feeling Alone

When people are fully engaged in community, no one will feel alone or lonely when by themselves.

Feeling alone or lonely is a symptom of unhealed shame. It is also a symptom of living in a culture dominated by toxic shame. The experience of feeling alone, which means not being connected in love and community, is difficult to see because we have so many ways of preventing ourselves from experiencing it.

"Alone" really means being away from who we are, taking on the definitions of others, believing the made up-world of those around us.

Authentic Need of Others

Living in community includes needing each other. Division of labor, having babies and bringing home food for the family has gone on over the centuries.

We have a need to be seen and the need to see others. Intimacy is a vital ingredient of being human, serving to create community that serves all. This is the kind of relating that we were designed to have. We require an honest reflection of ourselves and all of life in the eyes of others. We need to join in the task of creating and improving community. When we don't have this, we are alone, whether we experience it or not.

If true humanness means being needed for who we are, for being entirely ourselves, then we are all deprived. When I told a friend that I needed her to be herself, she was touched, because in her childhood she was needed and wanted only for what she did.

Having Children

Conceiving and having babies is a powerful way to access our human nature. It pulls us back into knowing how to come together as a couple, and create a family. This is one humanness that hasn't been completely lost because of shame. We still have to procreate in spite of shame. This instinct has been heavily distorted, but not lost.

Non-humans' Full Life Experience of Community

When living in Hawaii, I made friends with wild chickens. I watched them, saw how they addressed fear, and how they got over it. Gradually I interacted with them until I was able to lie on the ground and scoot toward a hen warming her brood under her wings. She let me touch the chicks without pecking me.

When I tamed chicks I could hold them on my hand while they ate. When I was relaxed and comfortable, they were glad to do this. But if I was even slightly tense, they would fly down. What an example of the ability of animals to know what is going on with others! Did they learn this from their feet on my hand, or was it a larger energy they perceived? We are prey as well as predators, don't we have this ability too? How was it squashed out of us? How can we reclaim it?

I also tamed wild cats. They don't hide their fear or their desire for love or their immense pleasure when able to feel safe on a lap. Each one came closer for a few days, then disappeared for a week or so, then returned for increasingly more intimate relating. Each cat repeated this for over a year until appearing more like house-raised domestic cats.

Brilliant yellow and green gold finches came to a feeder right outside my living room window. Colors flashed as they took turns, turning their heads in all directions while swallowing the seed they have picked out of the sock. Of course they are vigilant! They are prey. Prey have to pay attention to predators. They haven't been shamed into ignoring it. Their boundary is flight.

Myna birds in Hawaii gather at dusk and talk on and on as they move around in trees, swapping branches, until falling asleep at dark. They talk again on awakening. The huge banyan tree in Lahaina on Maui attracts thousands.

The albatross on the north shore of Kauai evolved with no predators, and so did not develop an instinctive fear of large animals. They express only mild concern when people walk right up to them.

None of these creatures lost their instinctive knowing of how to live. We can heal our way back to that.

Chapter 11: The Root of World Problems

Thinkers of all kinds have long tried to understand why our world is filled with violence, with blindness to the plight of others, and the ultimate abuse of humanness, war.

The reason is very simple. Shame. That intense unpleasantness that dominates every one of us and is passed along from generation to generation.

Toxic shame, that dreadful feeling of badness, of harming, of being unacceptable, of not belonging, of not being good enough brings stomach-clenching, skin-crawling sensations. It is something we all know, we all feel. It will quiet down, and then leap up when we're criticized or feel that we have done something wrong or stupid or harmful or against the rules. It can appear from just being alive.

As we prevent feeling shame, we limit our humanness, inhibiting our ability to live in peace, to easily solve conflicts, love children, develop our gifts and offer them to the community, and follow our instincts and intuition. As long as toxic shame is passed along in the culture, we as a people cannot fully find ourselves. We must know ourselves in order to identify our integrity and live appropriately.

We are left with an abbreviated version of humanity even while yearning for the full experience.

When we cut ourselves off from intuitive knowing of love and support and respect and community, then we can no longer see that killing in the name of righteous war is incompatible with our human instincts. Instead, we can justify anger and hitting others, including children. Rape and child molestation become easier because healthy shame and guilt go underground, becoming inaccessible.

Conscience is diminished. We live by habit instead of internally motivated integrity. Then we shame children without knowing we are harming.

As we medicate shame, it feels best when we join with others to do so. Gossip was invented for this function. The two of us against them.

Even more effective is when one country goes against other countries, judging and criticizing them for being different and strange. This evolves into nationalism, and racism, where those who appear one way condemn those who appear another. This makes us believe that we belong, that we are connected to a large number of people. The larger the number, the more right we feel, as our views are reflected back to us by so many. The larger the condemned group, the greater the effectiveness in warding off shame. When one whole group shames a whole other group, it is easy to rationalize being right.

The emotions that bind attackers become stronger when attacking physically. The other group will, of course, attack back in self defense. Then they, too, bond into a tight unit. Our "leaders" who start wars are offering up intense emotions that imitate intimacy. They hope to be valued for it. As physically abused children bind more tightly to abusive parents than do normal children, known as trauma bonding, war creates connection.

When we live outside of integrity, even more shame is added on. Then we must suffer even more distancing from our true knowing and humanness.

The avoidance of the experience of shame underpins much damaging behavior in our community: bad parenting, poor work cultures, argumentative marriages, crimes, and war. It is the cause of bad economies, of poverty, of passive-aggressive actions, of holding each other accountable for our difficulties, and practically anything in the news. It causes depression and anxiety and fear. It leads people to believe that solutions must include lying, stealing and taking advantage of each other.

Here's the wonderful thing. Shame can be healed! When it is, the world will be righted. War and domestic violence and harming children can be stopped!

If every person set out to heal shame by no longer shaming, no longer receiving shame, and by discharging the internalized forms, the world's population would get on track and live according to our communal instincts.

We are born full of love and life, with programming to discover our talents and gifts, and then develop them in ways that support community. We are capable of empathy, of seeing and being seen, of healing ourselves and others, of knowing how to be together without conflict. Shame is the pain that prevents us from accessing all of this. As I and my friends and clients heal our internalized toxic shame, we are discovering that it is possible to walk easily in the world, openly smiling and seeing and respecting others. Without internalized shame, we don't react to being shamed. Setting boundaries is effortless.

Chapter 12: Observations

Writing this book gave me a wonderful education. While I already understood most of what is in here, setting out to watch people and collect examples provided an amazing six months. As I put it all down in chapters, I found that there was more! So I put this cool stuff here in its own chapter.

Enjoying Being Alone

As an avoidant attacher, I have always enjoyed being by myself. However, because I was a dependent child, the use of this defense included needing the physical presence of adults but without interacting with them. Thus, going to restaurants, Starbucks, and grocery stores brought a comfortable sense of safety and belonging. People are all around, but I don't have to talk to anyone.

I used to deprive myself of this pleasure because I believed that people saw me as strange. When I became old enough to go to restaurants by myself, and then to travel alone, I was uncomfortable that others would think I was incapable of making friends or having a husband who wanted to be with me. As if the right choice was to be with others.

I didn't notice this shame until I began flying by myself. I loved long layovers. In an airport no one expected people to be with others! I could fit in and belong even while acting out my avoidant attachment.

As I wrote this, sitting alone at Starbucks, I watched an obese young woman with exceptionally large buttocks place her order. When she sat to wait for it, she had to pull the chair way out from the table to make room.

What must that be like? She cannot avoid shaming looks and comments. Most obese people believe that being thin will remove their shame and life will be good. It doesn't work for long. Only one kind of shame will be addressed.

Shameful Behaviors

A woman in a sports store showed me mouth guards. She said the one she uses to prevent grinding her teeth at night is best because it helped with drooling, then "admitted" that she drools, in the tone that invites me to smile with her to offset the shame. Why feel shame over bodily functions? Cultural rules.

One morning I was still in my bathrobe while I had breakfast. A man unexpectedly came to my door to do some work my contractor had ordered. I had to walk out to my gate to show him the problem. I was aware from the moment he knocked that I wasn't supposed to be in my bathrobe, but, out of character, I felt very little shame. My shame-healing is going well.

Why do we have rules about when you should bathe and dress? I think it's something like, you aren't doing anything useful or productive if not dressed. Or, you aren't living your life. In fact, I was living my life as fully as if I were dressed. I have to determine this for myself and not judge based on what others think. I imagined that he assumed I just sit around watching TV all day.

Some of my remaining sources of shame are showing up. My shame says that I am worthy of no shame if I work, if I don't waste time, if I don't watch TV during the day.

Here's another example of my shame. I noticed a whiny, victim-like tone when I told my racquetball partner that I hadn't gone to the challenge court while she was away. I checked in with my feelings, and saw that I was operating on the idea that if I were a truly committed player, I would have gone. I couldn't just acknowledge that I wasn't comfortable going without her and being the only woman/mediocre player. The men are friendly, nicely tolerant of us, and ratchet down their games to play with us.

Solutions for Healing

Every single one of us is shame-based solely because of living in a shame-based culture. Every one of us struggles to keep our shame at bay. Using defense mechanisms, criticizing, raging about nothing real, making objects of others, competing to win, excelling in school and work, being nice, taking care of others, and employing countless other maneuvers result in everyone around us, and ourselves, not being present and fully alive. This was the last layer of denial I had to rip off, and it is still ripping. Removing this denial is necessary in order to complete healing from shame.

To give up my methods of avoiding toxic shame, first I need to recognize how I do it.

We must identify and study all those ways that we use to stop feeling shame, believing that it really isn't there. Falling in love is popular because for a brief time we are looked at intensely with caring and acceptance. We are seen as shameless and good. Love is blind, right? Yes. We are perfect in the eyes of the beloved until enough time has passed and the illusion falls apart. Then comes the shaming, the hurt from being seen as deserving shame, and the horror of losing our source of sidestepping shame. We feel betrayed.

I motioned the person to go at the four-way stop at the same time he motioned me to do the same. We smiled, and I went. I took pleasure in this generosity. When I drove on, I realized that we both got to feel like good people, and we both got to receive appreciation from the other for being good. We felt connected. Perhaps this was a genuine caring for each other and wanting to make things go smoothly. It may also have been a method to avoid shame by feeling good about ourselves.

My confidence in my intuition grows the more I strip off denial of how extensive shame avoidance is. It can feel genuinely good when someone does something for me, yet other times it is clear that the person is only trying to get affirmation. Before I trusted my intuition, a gas station attendant in cold Alaska offered to check the pressure in my tires just as I was about to do it. As soon as he began, I knew that I was supposed to walk around the car, appreciating each tire. Instead, I got in my car to stay warm, the only reason to accept his offer. Driving off, I wished I had done it myself so that I would have lived the truth. I had let him do it because I didn't want to seem rude, saying no to a kind gesture. But as Bradshaw says, being kind is actually hateful. It set him up to hate me for not responding as I was supposed to. It set me up to look ungrateful if I said no. And if I said yes.

We all want to fit in and belong. But if we follow the rules for medicating everyone's shame, we truly don't fit in and can't belong in any connected way.

Walking through several malls, I looked at people. I used to believe that most of those around me were happy and had satisfying lives. Even when I began practicing as a psychologist, I thought my clients and I were the exceptions. We were the ones with problems unlike "normal" people. My magical thinking thought that I could be like them if only I completed some magical process.

That lie sustained me. Perhaps in childhood it truly did sustain me. I lived in fantasy, imagining the adult life I could have as soon as I was old enough. Only now do I recognize my fantasy that people around me had comfortable, loving, meaningful lives with only occasional external stresses. I thought that anger and shaming and other harmful behaviors were either appropriate, or the person exhibiting them was crazy.

I now grasp the truth that every single one of us was harmed in childhood. And that all of us struggle with how to handle internalized toxic shame.

This makes me angry. As I walked among the people in the malls, I raged over the isolation each one is living. This raging pulled off another layer of denial, letting me see this tragedy more clearly. I have more raging, and more denial pulling-off to do. It has been incredibly difficult to see how alone everyone is.

Here is the amazing benefit of knowing how separate people are. Nothing other people do is surprising. Never again comes the question, why did he do that? If the behavior seems irrational, or unexpected, or dramatic, or even crazy, you will know that this person has discovered this way to avoid feeling as if he or she isn't worth being alive. Or, his methods don't work and he feels the horror of very old shame.

A man was disliked by his neighbors because he was an angry, vengeful person. After a few months of my speaking to him in a friendly way, he became angry when I built a small building on my property, reported every suspected infraction to the county, came on my property to inspect it, and damaged things in small ways. He lied to my workers about things I had done. The construction foreman was upset, and wanted to triangulate with me against this bad person. I didn't join him. I didn't believe this man would do anything truly destructive, he was causing trouble in the name of righteousness. He has truly horrible ways of avoiding his shame.

Being Hated

When my client glared at me hatefully I knew it was because I looked him in the eyes and said I know he is lying. He hates me instead of feeling shame.

Another client angrily told me she wasn't coming back. Her shame was triggered, too. She wanted support to stay in her old patterns.

In the past I tried to make the other person feel better and not think I was harmful. I wanted to medicate shame. This was stressful because it failed. I could never figure out exactly what the person needed, of course, because I can't heal someone's shame for them.

It's not stressful when I am able to stand back watching someone work hard to avoid feeling shame. I can see that raging and criticizing and gossiping and triangulating against others are unreal mechanisms to feel temporarily better. It is always temporary.

A vital outcome of seeing is that I don't have to shame others!

As I heal my own shame, I don't have to shame others in order to medicate my own. As I am more present to the truth, I can see more clearly that they don't deserve shaming and criticism. It is meaningless. Criticizing others shamingly even in my head was such a barrier to being in the present.

If I'm making things up I am not in the present.

It's powerful to be angry when necessary, and to firmly point out the truth when someone is harming. But that is all there is to it. Shaming doesn't motivate people to make real changes.

While I am becoming freer, others can be uncomfortable with the truth even when I deliver it in a non-shaming manner. A friend began drinking heavily after a life trauma, and recognized that she is an alcoholic, but she had difficulty stopping. I said, in a calm caring tone, that her teenage son was harmed by her addiction. This was painful, and elicited a great deal of shame. I believe that if I had shamed her for it, it would have been less painful because her long practiced defenses would have leaped into gear and held off the shame.

Winning

One of the foremost values of our culture is that winning is better than losing. If you lose, then you have to be a good sport about it. In other words, you can't express the shame and upset over not getting to use this method of being shame-free and happy.

If you don't win, the next value is doing your best. Then you are acceptable. Why do your best? Isn't enjoying yourself good enough? In fact, if we were shame free, enjoying ourselves would be the primary reward.

A shame-free culture would support each person in finding his or her interests, talents, what mental or physical makeup assists the ability, what feels good. When learning how to be a therapist I confronted shame over inadequacy, but along with that was a fascination that propelled me to become good at it. I didn't do my best in order to meet the requirements of a shame-based culture. I was interested, I put in time, and lo and behold, I became good at it!

I healed from unconsciously directed failure to win at competitive games. When playing racquetball with someone at my level, I used to lose more than win. If I got ahead I would suddenly not be able to play well. I couldn't control this, but eventually the healing process allowed me to play my best. I won most games by a large score difference. As I continued to win point after point I felt separate. I was alone. I was isolated.

I haven't yet learned the reasons for this isolation, but healing shame also allowed me to claim being visible when winning. I became comfortable while being watched as I played, too. It made no difference at all. Shame down, life up!

When I completed my Ph. D. I opened a nice office, had supportive colleagues, a new car, new professional clothes, a lovely home, and a family. I wore a very old watch with pieces chipping off. I didn't want a new watch. I clung to the physical evidence that everything in life wasn't perfect. I hadn't entirely won.

Limited Intimacy

We do have intimacy, of course. If we didn't, life would seem valueless.

When living in Hawaii, I frequently visited a beach that a river rearranged several times each winter, then sand would be replaced by the ocean. I loved watching the rapid geological changes. One day I was walking along the wild river marveling at its effects when a man passed me, smiled, and said, "Incredible, isn't it?" I said, "Yes!" We had a perfect moment of shared pleasure. Intimacy.

People in combat share real intimacy because it is necessary for survival. They need to see each other's needs and meet them in a communing, team-work manner. Human instincts motivate us to meet real needs. Our own and those of others.

Television shows and movies use intense situations in their plots in order to offer us something we really want to feel. When we identify with the actors, we get to have that uplifting emotion of being entirely occupied with being human and with the needs of those around us. Shows based on medical issues, or violent trauma, or the danger of death to the main character, or preventing someone from being killed, grabs us by our humanness. It takes this kind of intensity to pull us away from our shame-based choices of how to act. We get to live in our humanness for a short while.

I sometimes cry in front of my TV. When watching these characters having powerful experiences that require their entire humanness, I grieve for the lack of it. As my denial pulls loose, I can see why these shows feel good. Now, instead of joining in a false life with the characters, I grieve for the very need to have these scenes! I appreciate how good writing and acting can take us into these very feelings that we are designed to have. We get the satisfaction of using our humanness. How tragic that we want to experience this through the medium of acting, portrayed on a cold screen! If we were shame free, and lived fully in community, the substitute humanity of television would hold little interest.

Following politics beyond obtaining information and deciding what to do creates another way for people to engage in what feels like human community. In real life, being ER doctors and nurses, 911 dispatchers, EMT in ambulances, and firefighters are career choices that allow people occupied by the very real needs of others to disengage their shame for a time. This feels especially good to those who live with shame.

Offering Intimacy Everywhere

I have come to see the ways in which I avoid shame, feel abused, and join in non-intimate relating. Every time I went to a grocery store, bank, or Starbucks, I watched how the checker or barista acted and how I acted. My friend who used to work in a grocery store explained that checkers are burned out by customers treating them like servants to be shamed, or seen as nonexistent! Why would I expect that they would see me and think there was a chance that I would be different?

I appreciate my automatic commitment to healing, my Feet, as they got me to study shame, and then become different. I had already known that my avoidant attachment needed examination in order for me to release it. Looking at the pervasiveness of shame all around us, being able to accept people as they are, insisting on living with truth, and seeing that I had accepted my mother's shaming by the very process of proving her wrong, moved me to grasp how I can offer myself anywhere. I mustn't wait around until I find people who are capable of intimacy! What an absurd approach to finding humanness! (I am not shaming myself. Absurdity is real. It doesn't imply shame-worthy.)

Living the Truth

Shame gets us to lie, to deceive, and to withhold information to avoid being shamed by others. It prevents the intimacy that requires revealing ourselves.

If we heal shame we will automatically tell the truth.

Deceiving causes us to feel shame. It supports the very shame we are trying to medicate with deception. One way to heal shame is to learn how we are deceiving, and then experiment with stopping.

We create boundaries against being shamed. Without full access to our humanness, we have difficulty knowing what good boundaries are, what boundaries are really needed. On the phone, my client tells his father that he has to meet with a customer when the truth is that he is bored hearing the same stories over and over. He can't tell his father that he heard the story before, and could they talk about something of interest to both of them. This would be a self-caring, non-shaming solution.

If the father reacted predictably, and shamed my client for these comments, the son could let the father know that he isn't to criticize anymore. Period. Then wait to see what happens next. The father may want to hang up, or shame some more, or apologize. My client doesn't know, because he has never set boundaries to find out.

I do know from years of working with clients that the father will change. Not an internal, healing change, but a behavioral one. He will grasp that the system has changed. His son has changed. He will have to act differently in order to continue relating. This is all my client needs. To have his boundaries respected.

The first task when telling the truth is knowing what the truth is. Dishonesty is more than obvious lies or secrets. I have practiced perceiving what is going on with others for years, and naming both that and what is going on inside of me. But of course this is only practical with close friends who agree that they want this kind of revelation, and with clients who pay me to tell them. Sad to say, hearing my observations can bring shame even while I am truly not shaming. The very needed awareness and communication provoke shame associations from the past and from the culture. We all want intimacy, but being seen is frightening because we fear our badness will be seen too. And of course it is. If it weren't for the dreadful experience of shame, we would want to know how we are harmful so we can change!

For a long time I assumed that I couldn't tell the whole truth to strangers or acquaintances. But now I see that if I hold myself back, I make myself alone. So I am venturing out to see what to do when the grocery clerk asks me how I am and I know he really doesn't care.

After decades of learning how not to lie, I came to see that I have to give up every bit of lying. The very day I was pondering this I played racquetball on a court that I was to use only when with a person who lived in the complex. Our court was being refinished and my partner and I didn't want to stop playing for two weeks. We couldn't find other options that didn't include becoming members of a club. My friend who lived in the complex unlocked the door of the court for us two times, but the third he was out of town. We went anyway, hoping a court had been left open. It hadn't.

When I asked a member if he would open the door he looked at me strangely, explaining that the key to the outside door would do it. Now here is where in the distant past I might have wanted to say my friend was late and he had the key. Even when I didn't lie, I always felt a little shame about doing something wrong, and wanting somehow to make the person think I wasn't. But this time I told the whole, absolute truth. I didn't look down or away. I said that we didn't live here, and my friend who did isn't here to open the door. Done. My energy flowed forward toward the person.

The man responded with the desire to meet a real need, which had been presented in an honest, real way. He had no interest in judging me for using the court without my friend present.

I loved the open, fluid feeling this brought. It seemed like the best reward for refusing to distort things, for being fully committed to telling the truth. I didn't do it for him. I did it so that I got to stay with myself, alive.

Two men on the other court did the opposite. I asked them if they could open the door for us, and they explained that they didn't have a key, that their friend had unlocked the door, left, and was coming back, but they weren't sure when. I asked about how long, and they said twenty minutes. I said I would wait. Later I realized that they were lying! The friend wasn't coming back. In fact, he didn't. How must they have felt at the thought of my sitting in the hall waiting for their friend! Luckily, I went on to find someone in the workout room for the key. This is like the plot of so many sitcoms where lies create all kinds of difficulties.

One racquetball afternoon I was feeling low, almost depressed, and playing didn't bring me out of it as it usually did. My partner didn't seem herself either, and I wondered if she had picked up on my mood. So I stopped to tell her about it. She said she wondered if I were reacting to her series of bad shots! Her next thought was wondering if it were her outfit. We laughed together over the automatic assessment of the other person's mood as being caused by oneself, and the shame that is so tightly interwoven! I felt better after telling her.

I wouldn't have been lying or deceiving or even withholding a truth if I hadn't said anything. But relating in a shame-ridden culture requires revealing ourselves to those who can understand, accept, and join us in humanness.

I tell the truth as soon as I know what it is. The hard part is knowing what it is.

Being Well-Adjusted

Well-adjusted doesn't mean mentally healthy. It doesn't mean living in integrity. Well-adjusted people have adjusted to the cultural shaming and resulting lying. Those who don't want to adjust struggle with not fitting in and not belonging.

Fear of Healing from Shame

While I think that we are happier when we give up old shame and our defenses against it, it is truly difficult and awkward, even frightening to give up shame. Toxic shame is the foundation of the culture. It is the basis of our identity. It is the foundation of most of our choices for how to spend time and how to relate with one another. Even pleasant, productive and caring behaviors can be designed to avoid feeling shame.

Change Is Frightening

I am often asked why people change so slowly once they understand why they feel bad. Some forms of psychotherapy address the client's beliefs, because when we change what we believe, the resulting unpleasant emotions, including shame, change, too. For example, if a woman believes that she is defective for failing a college class, the therapist can help her change her belief about the meaning of failing, which will change her resulting emotions. She can stop feeling defective. But this doesn't address the deeply held traumas and the shame that has been placed on us by history and culture. When we change our very identity, we need to grieve. And when the grief has had its effect, then operating in new ways requires an adjustment.

As my fear of being evil dissolved, I consistently woke feeling alive and ready for the day. As each piece fell, going out in public was more interesting. But after a few days of this, I noticed that I was feeling afraid! All this change was unfamiliar.

Fear of change shows up other ways, too. I can sit in my living room with a vague sense of danger, but with nothing to attribute it to. I might make up what it's about, but quickly realize that that isn't it. There are no solutions to this fear. It helps to know that it is either fear of change, or it is fear that I grew up with. Then I know that it is part of a process, and it will pass when I have discharged it sufficiently.

Facing fear of change is part of change.

Right along with shame and fear of shame and fear of anything else, the emotion needs space for its discharge. I let the sensation in my chest flow and I consciously breathe.

It is helpful to think about my identity, my ways of viewing myself and the world, and my avoidant attachment, as life-saving. While they didn't actually save my life, they did make me feel safe from dying. Something that I believed was saving my life would be very frightening to stop! So of course I will feel terror along with the old shame, intermixed with the grief to let the past go.

This state of fear and shame and grief all flowing together needs to be tolerated in order to complete the grief and leave the past in the past.

Lisa understood that when she took care of her baby granddaughter, she would feel badly the next day. The baby is happy and full of life in contrast to the misery Lisa felt with a mother who didn't want her. The contrast brings up this information for Lisa to experience, which is painful. She no longer needs the life-saving defenses of self-shaming and doubting what she knows.

Sticks and Stones

Why is it humiliating when your partner has sex with someone else? Naturally it would feel bad, angering, frightening, threatening of the security of the relationship. Communing would be lost. But humiliation? That comes from seeing the relationship as meaning something about each person's worth and value. These are shame-laden ideas.

Self-esteem is one of those terms that is supposed to be the opposite of shame. It means that you feel good about yourself. If we were all shame-free we wouldn't have a term like self-esteem in our vocabulary. It is what causes people to look to the outside for approval and acceptance instead of looking at themselves to see how it is right to live life. Esteem is sought in order to offset shame. It is not a genuine result of healing shame. Self-esteem is on the opposite end of the measuring stick from self-condemnation. Both are self judgments of our worth.

Bodily Shame

My son was disgusted when I put essential oils on Q tips and put them in my nose for twenty minutes to heal a chronic infection. If there were no cultural shaming, wouldn't he think it looked really funny? His sons would think that. They haven't had adult training in disgust yet.

I have used coffee enemas for years to detoxify my body and help my liver do a better job of this important task. Coffee enemas are a popular alternative healing practice for cancer, and for those of us who want to stay healthy as long as possible, yet no one talks about it because of shame regarding bowel movements.

Nose hair, pimples, underarm sweat, hairstyles ruined by sudden rain, dirty fingernails, small penises or breasts, fat, body shape less than ideal, and a thousand other small characteristics of how we actually are will bring shame. Even when we do it all right, we still shame ourselves by the very belief that we have to do it right.

Recognition of Shame

Giving up the idea that there are mentally healthy people in the world makes room to understand that, every man, woman and child is carrying shame, differing only in degree. And every one of us is medicating it. The amount of shame is on a continuum from just cultural to deeply felt in every cell of the being. The medication of that shame is described in Chapter 7. On the far end are those who are in such deep pain that they resort to deadly addictions. If addictions don't work to dampen the pain, then depression takes over.

I have a friend who forgives people when they do things he finds objectionable. He gave the example of a driver cutting him off. As he became angry, he cut it short by forgiving the driver. This does allow him to stop feeling angry. However, if he healed some of his shame he wouldn't find himself angry. Then he would have nothing to forgive.

Being hated can be tolerated when one is shame-free.

When I had a lot of shame I didn't like being around people who hated me. Years ago I went into a two-week depression when a client coldly condemned me in front of group members. This was beyond my reactions to criticism, because if someone criticized I could defend myself, showing that they were wrong. If someone hated me, especially if they didn't tell me why, I would become disorganized and be unable to think clearly. I had to end a relationship with a client who hated me and couldn't process it. I would attempt to engage her caring side, but always knew that hatred was waiting in the wings.

This disorganized reaction was projected from childhood where my mother's hatred threatened my life more than once. In order to avoid her hatred, I learned all the rules and followed them. I didn't believe that the rules were correct, but I did believe that I had better follow them for safety. So even when someone hates me in a withheld, sort of kindly, manner, I react in the same life-preserving way I learned in childhood.

With my shame reduced, I can understand that hating me is only a maneuver for that person to avoid feeling terrible. That's okay. It's not about me.

The Avoidant Defense Against Shame

Those of us who use avoidant attachment as a defense feel isolated and alone, cut off from others. When asked if I feel lonely, I always say no. The sense of isolation goes way beyond lonely. It's being so isolated that lonely isn't even possible. Loneliness is the experience of missing those you like to be around, or needing people so that talking even with strangers relieves it. When engaged in avoidant attachment, I yearn for something human, some permanent presence of others. But it can't be just anyone. Friendships won't fulfill this need that is based in history.

When I am "gone," as we call it, I have little awareness of the world around me. I don't see beauty and color, I don't smile and drink in the beauty of the red leaves on the poinsettia I saved from the year before, or the bright yellow hibiscus flowers contrasting with the green lawn and foliage. I am occupied by a physical sensation that might be called anxiety except that it isn't like the kind that comes with real situations. It's an old, deadened sensation. I have little experience of life, even while preparing a meal or feeding the animals. I am not motivated to do anything, carrying out only rote tasks.

I am grateful that I rarely return to that deep isolation.

Samples Of Ordinary Shame

We take for granted that others will feel embarrassed when doing something against the rules. Standing in line at the drugstore I overheard a very old woman in front of me say to the clerk, "My husband would kill me if I paid too much." The clerk, trying to be kind, said, "I don't think your husband would kill you." The customer said, "He can't because he's already dead." She had dementia. The clerk apologized! After the woman left, the clerk said to me that she should think before she speaks!

As the observer, I can see that the clerk has nothing to apologize for.

As a student of shame, I could see that the customer hadn't intended to cause shame or defensiveness. I made up that she had repeated that line for decades. She is keeping her husband alive with her sayings. But when the clerk referred to her husband, she then knew that he was dead. Her brain wasn't working well enough to apologize to the clerk.

Backlash from Healing

It is necessary to expect days of up and down. The down is essential to heal the past and make life even better. I don't like this, but I understand it. I am willing, and my Feet tell me this is the path. Better to know that we are going to go up and down so we can tolerate it more easily. I have never known anyone, client or friend, who didn't go to the down place during healing. I warn people about it when they have reached a new high. I don't want them to think that the high wasn't real.

It also helps me to know that giving up old ways of being is going to bring a strong emotional reaction. We developed methods to avoid shame and annihilation and abandonment, so when we stop using them, we are bound to fear that these very experiences are impending. This can be quite dramatically challenging. After going through it enough times, I associate an intense negative reaction with positive change. So instead of feeling badly for having it, and worrying about its significance, I value its significance! Is that reverse psychology??

Avoidant Attachment Shames

Avoidant attachment shames others. I am judging others as not worthy of my relating. I believe others are evaluating me in the same manner. As my shame drops, I am becoming able to open my hand to everyone. If a hand reaches back, wonderful. If it doesn't, I am safe with my boundaries.

Avoidant attachment breeds fear of shame. The dominating belief is that I am entirely responsible for myself, can't ask for help, and can't have it. This is because I am alone. I imagine that people with poor social skills have avoidant attachment style. We didn't learn them while growing up. I developed some when in college, but before that, I was outside, quietly listening.

When I think about what not relating would do to a person's sense of safety in community, I realize why avoidant attachers need to be self-sufficient. If natural relating is communing with others in a mutual need-meeting way, then we would of course feel shame for our failure to do that and terror from not having the safety it brings. Our primitive minds can't let us know when communing is possible and when it's not. Shame has to be out of the way to understand.

So I am healing shame in order to heal avoidant attachment in order to have as much love and communing as possible!

As a recovering avoidant attacher I am learning about all the ways people will interact with me now that I am open to everyone. While I have been enjoying bits and pieces with strangers, I am also learning how little communing there is. My healing alternates between joyfully seeing how much I've been missing and sadly grieving for the absence.

I ponder the role of shame experienced by people with different attachment styles. Is it perhaps true that secure attachment would bring more internalized family requirements and cultural rules that make people feel shame? If they fit in and belonged they might feel compelled to accept "normal" shaming. And would avoidant attachment only include the shame made up about oneself? Would the typical avoidant attacher believe he or she had some basic evil that accounts for receiving so much abuse and neglect?

A pigeon walked by and I appreciated its iridescent feathers and beautiful, complex patterning. Yet these birds are shamed for moving in, procreating in great numbers, and pooping on everything. They are shamed based on what humans want. Other birds by the lake or the ocean are seen as wonderful and interesting. They don't bother us. I find them interesting, but I have to sneak up on them, using binoculars to get a good look. The beautiful pigeon brings herself right here to me!

Stopping Some Stimuli

Ongoing stimulation, like having the radio and television on all the time, distract from what would emerge. Setting aside times with no distractions in order to see what shows up might reveal emotions that would appear if not avoided. Giving up phoning, texting, e-mailing. Doing nothing but sitting in the yard, going to the beach. Drinking only water, nothing with alcohol, caffeine, or other mood changers. See what happens.

Decades ago I always had the radio on when driving and music or television playing at home. One day I stopped wanting the stimulation. Now I can see that Feet wanted me to pay attention to myself. Sometimes I will listen to NPR as I'm driving. Sometimes I turn it on when I am tired of feeling what I am feeling! It can be interesting to notice how my unpleasant emotion might still be there, but when I have something else to pay attention to, I don't find it as unpleasant. It has taken Feet's commitment to healing to get me to stop distracting myself.

Shame-Free Curiosity

Studying shaming going on all around us is a powerful way to lift denial. Talking about other people is usually in the vein of how silly-stupid-incompetent-mean they are. This imprints our own shame more deeply even while in the service of not feeling it for a while.

Going out in public with my computer lets me observe countless examples of shaming. If I listen with curiosity, my denial lifts. I see how ordinary situations such as sitting in a coffee shop reveal the culture's illness.

I sat near two men, one dressed in clothing that was to indicate wealth. He told the other man how his tailor in San Francisco had suits he knew he would like, he could walk in and be fitted in ten minutes, and the suits would be ready before he got on the plane back home. Then he talked about the different experiences of driving various expensive cars.

This man lives in great shame. Instead of believing that he was successful and thus happy, I knew that being far better dressed and wealthy did nothing to heal his shame. It may have medicated it. But even this wasn't successful or he wouldn't have had to show this acquaintance how well he does.

A few years ago I would have criticized him for bragging. But if I do, I can't see how miserable he is.

Another well-dressed young man sat slumped over, the clothing not able to create an impression. When two older men arrived in shirt sleeves, it was obvious that he was applying for something from them. A job or sale of a product. Shame made him miserable. It made him look very different from the two men he was with.

An hour later a man about fifty walked by me and sat in the next chair. I could feel his energy. He was desperately sucking on mine. He had to be an anxious attacher. I almost moved so I could concentrate on writing, but then a younger man joined him. I was not surprised when he showed false happiness and talked in a victim voice. Shame-based.

I did not observe any low-shame people during those several hours of writing. I rarely do.

Anger When Healing

I have periods of free-floating anger while grieving. Today is one of those. Again in Starbucks, writing and observing.

I'm angry because I'm shame free! First I want to give up shame. Then I'm afraid of giving it up. And when it's gone, I'm mad! This is the alternating between the wonderful benefits of shame healing and the backlash into the old beliefs and emotions that we are releasing.

This makes intellectual sense, but on the inside it feels really really stupid!

Why do we cling to shame? This is the question that has to do with fear of change. I have an identity based on my way of defending myself against shame. While my experience of shame isn't as strong as for many, it still limits me. I have a pleasure quota. I limit the amount of time I spend in a freely joyful, shame-free place. It has to do with maintaining the familiar methods of handling my mother's view of me as evil by shutting down and being very still. If I stop using those methods, then what?

Feet often struggle against Anti-Feet, who argue for shame. The struggle feels safe, whereas no struggle catapults me out into the world, able to take on anything, anytime. This is why change takes so long. Even when I have changed so much, I limit my experience of it. Backlash.

While I was writing about anger, a woman sat next to me and asked if I was writing a book. We had an animated conversation about what each of us does, and when she left I saw a shame-free reflection of me. I am writing a book in Starbucks. I exist. I had continued to see this as a shame-worthy scene instead of something very ordinary. At the same time, I have defended against that shame. Now that I can see it more clearly, I see what an absolute waste of energy this is! It's really stupid (said in a non-shaming way).

My identity includes being weird, strange, odd, and out of the norm. It also includes being interesting, provocative, and focused on unusual things. These views of myself have been seamless, so I didn't realize that clinging to being myself included clinging to the view of being weird and different!

Still at Starbucks, two men are talking in what I would call a superior victim style, telling stories about people who have stupidly unfair practices. I smile. I had thought that the whole world was like that. Yet the successful business woman talked with me right here in public, amid ordinary people of the world with no shaming of anyone! A cross-section of people walks through here. I get to be one of them!

A woman knocked a cup off the table and it broke. When the worker came to sweep it up she apologized in shame. The man nearest her jokingly said that it was made by the emperor of China. Everyone laughed to help her override shame. This is a kind, acceptable method of helping someone not feel it. This has been going on forever. And will go on forever.

I wonder if all people with avoidant attachment would expect shaming from others. Perhaps this is the reason we avoid. People with anxious attachment still believe that something good could be coming and are willing to risk it. These people would perhaps learn more social skills in order to get what they can. We avoiders don't need social skills, but feel shame for not being able to fit in and belong. It is a protective defense to feel apart, even while knowing that it is a wrong way to live. Giving it up brings fear of what would have happened if I had never avoided. I would have been shamed to death. I avoided shame by avoiding attachment.

My mother looked at me with hatred even when she acted caring. I always knew it was an act. Even when I was in the hospital after an appendectomy when I was thirteen years old, and she came every day. I was glad she did, because staying there for five days was really strange. She brushed my hair, which was the only way she could have physical contact with me. This seemed consistent with her attitude, but many years later I saw that she was only able to hug anyone when clenching her arms to her sides, extending only her forearm. She never hugged us growing up. Now I can see that she had been physically shamed. She passed that onto us by finding us unpleasant to touch. Of course we took this to mean that it was something about us.

By avoiding attachment I could pretend that the world was over there, and I was over here. I could compartmentalize the shaming to that distant arena. I could learn about myself over here.

After writing that, I sobbed out loud. I cried for the fact that I hadn't been loved. I had known this intellectually, but now I was immersed in the true knowing that I needed and deserved love and that, instead, my mother's face looked at me through a veil of hate and condemnation.

Section 2 Healing From Shame

I have listed some basic approaches to healing this emotion out of ourselves. My book, *Love Against Shame: A Five Step Practice for Claiming Self-esteem* offers life experiences of myself, clients and friends as a guide for walking through an actual practice to remove shame from our minds, bodies and spirits. It takes what is here, and lots more, weaving it through easy to comprehend stories. It will help you enter the new sub-culture of a shame free environment so you can change your perceptions of how you get to live.

Chapter 13: Find a Shame Healing Group

In therapy sessions I am one individual person who listens intently with empathy and compassion, and who accepts my client. While this is helpful for those who haven't been able to reveal shameful experiences, when she gives the same information to a group who listen the same way, the effect of reducing shame is magnified many times over.

Can you imagine telling a group of people something you've never been able to talk about, and see six caring, compassionate faces looking right back at you? People who carry their own shame and fear of revealing it? This is one of the functions of 12-step groups based on Alcoholics Anonymous. As each member accepts the other members, that acceptance is reflected back to him or her.

In Healing Sexual Shame workshops women move from fearfully wanting to say nothing to eagerly waiting until they can talk. It is comforting to grasp that others have similar experiences and emotions.

As men come to trust other men in group therapy, they admit to behaviors they thought they would never tell anyone. The surprise is that almost every time that happens, more than one other man has the same shameful story. As men heal their shame they become capable of empathy and intimacy, sometimes for the very first time.

Options for Shame-Healing

•Shame is stronger when revealed to others. Because of this, writing what you are thinking and feeling might be the first step. Just write it down in order to take it outside yourself. Reading to someone what you wrote will help even more.

•The next level is finding friends who want to heal shame together. Three or four of you can study acculturated shaming and use this book as a guide.

As members are in agreement about the harm of shame, and study together how it appears all around us all the time, you will be in a group with those who learn to see things that are not seen by typical Americans.

Adopting these new understandings by yourself can feel isolating. Doing so with friends is better.

Go to movies and malls and restaurants and coffee shops and family gatherings, the shame classrooms. Study the evidence of shame.

Join others on webinars or videoconferencing groups in order to connect with people doing the same kind of shame healing. For more information, go to http://www.annestirlinghastings.com. I have colleagues to assist with shame associated with LGBTQ. The videoconferencing site is HIPAA approved.

Shame Healing Group

Therapy groups begin with topics that might have contributed to early shame. Some examples are, what was going on with your parents when you were born? How did you experience their love as a toddler? What losses and separations did you have before age five? How did your parents' religious values convey shame? What was your earliest memory of inadequate parenting? How do you feel shame in your body? How do you avoid feeling shame?

Responses and the emotions that come with them are welcomed and respected. Grief that may free one of historical shame is encouraged. Learning the skills of shame healing is primary.

I am grateful when groups soften as each person talks. Those who were tense and reserved can become eager. Everyone feels shame, but with many pairs of non-shaming eyes, it doesn't hurt as much! Knowing that everyone else feels it when they are talking, too, brings a sense of togetherness in this project. Each one sees that the other person is not bad. This is mirrored back as they experience being a member of the community. If no one else is bad, then you aren't either.

Chapter 14: Observation

When we can see, denial lifts, we grieve, and we change! It's as simple as that. Observe! Learn how to see cultural shaming, self shaming, childhood shaming, and how we are shamed every day.

Don't *make* yourself change!

Culturally supported methods of change involve setting out to make it happen, and shaming ourselves into it. This won't work.

Shaming yourself
will work against stopping the
shaming of yourself.

This is why I emphasize setting out to observe, and observe only. Trust that seeing increasingly clearly will automatically bring about emotional change. Trying to stop shaming will only add more shame.

While having a goal of change can actually prevent change, engaging in a practice is useful. This would include meeting regularly with others and setting aside study time. There is no success, or failure, at conducting a practice. There are no tests for the amount learned or skills mastered!

The solution to changing your life is all in the practice of observing.

We offer video conferencing and webinars so you will have an easy way to interact with others addressing their shame.

Observe without Shaming

If you engage with feeling critical of people for how they exhibit their shame, you will inhibit your education. You will shame yourself, too, which will make it hard to take a look at how you are doing just what the other person is doing.

Observe with Compassion

It may be hard to have compassion in the beginning, as seeing people shaming each other is something the culture shames! If a parent tells a child that she is stupid, and don't ever do that again, don't we look at each other with the expression of, "Oh my god, how could she say that to the little girl?" We are doing to her exactly what she did to the child.

As with the entire study of shame, observe your desire to shame people. Don't stop. Just notice. How does it feel? What would it feel like if you didn't shame others? What is it like to shame with co-healers? What is it like if none of you shames? This information can help you open up to internally motivated, automatic change.

Observe Automatic Change after Shame Drops

Now you can have a very pleasurable observation! While healing shame I encountered instances that seem to have nothing to do with shame, but are. When shame is down we don't have to defend against it. You may find gossip less interesting. I discovered being able to experience a warm loving sensation in my body that diminishes when memory-shame emerges.

A woman became able to ask questions in airports and stores and felt freer to move in the world. A man no longer felt dependent on his wife's approval, and was able to leave a well-paying job for one that he loved. I found that I could more easily see who, of the people I ran into, were able to have wonderful brief exchanges. A co-healer discovered that she could just look at her husband when he shamed her, without defending herself and entering into their classic circular argument. When he got no response he stopped.

Shame allows us to hurt ourselves, whether that's as simple as diet or as complex as addictions and depression and suicide.

The ability to see, which means removing denial, increases more rapidly when done with others. Once I could recognize that shame allowed me to ignore my body's nutritional needs, I told my co-healers. This helped them realize that their selections of unhealthy food were caused by shame, too.

When a client learned how to stop receiving his wife's shaming, he stopped using his usual method of getting judgmentally angry in order to not feel shame. He told his friends. His story made it easier for them to recognize when they received shaming and how they, too, stopped themselves from feeling it.

Observe with Understanding

Being able to understand when people are defending against their shame offers freedom. No longer do you have to react, feel defensive, prove them wrong, or feel shame when defenses don't work.

The best defense is
understanding

A friend and I experienced an example of the difference. A server came to our table and acted out the part of a made-up lovely person who was very interested in us. I could see she was in great emotional pain.

I asked my co-healer what she had observed, and when she said she didn't like the woman, I asked her to reflect on why the woman acted like this. Immediately she saw the level of shame underlying the behavior. Then she could join me in extending a sense of compassion, an energetic acceptance and sympathy.

Talking about it made the experience more real. We could together extend love. By sharing, we added to our understanding of why people develop false selves. By seeing clearly, we didn't respond to the false self. I didn't do the expected smiles and head nodding. Instead I looked at our server seriously, reflecting her real self back to her. I don't know if this was useful, but I got to offer her something different from those who believe the presentation. And this is better for me.

When out in the world, observing with a couple of co-healers, you might invent what you think people are experiencing. Don't worry about accuracy. Look at the woman in the grocery store who is impatient with her children. Perhaps she is afraid her husband is having an affair, or they can't pay the mortgage. What shame might she be abating? How often does she speak to them this way? Your stories will become increasingly accurate as you learn how to perceive. A great deal of information is available as you remove the inhibitions created by shame. When we can't know ourselves, we can't know the stories of others. But as we claim ourselves, developing the ability to have our emotions, including shame, we can see so much more! The best education is right in front of us. We can become able to perceive what is occurring everywhere.

It is possible to continually heal shame and become able to understand the motivations of those around us. Developing the ability to observe with understanding is powerful.

Memory

We can help emotional change by observing our false feelings and beliefs alongside present true ones. All of us, not only combat veterans, have flashbacks, but they vary in intensity. Those physically abused will have body memory and dreams that are conditioned from earlier life. Bringing up old fears, as combat vets do, offers a chance to discover that the fear is no longer needed as the person is no longer in combat. This realization is not intellectual, in the same way that the loss of someone to death isn't completed by understanding. Both require emotional grieving.

Attachment deprivation and conclusions based on it also require an emotional process to heal them into the past. Dreams and emotional flashbacks can assist this, but if not understood as productive, they are seen as uncomfortable, meaningless events.

By setting out to stop using some of our defenses against feeling shame, we offer freedom to these old areas that need healing. When I removed some of my defenses I confronted night walking terrors, hearing people in the house, and feeling as if I were dead. I met with co-healers almost every day, and grieved my way through the process. In a few weeks, I felt wonderfully alive. Since that time I have approached this defense removal, and healing of what appeared, in smaller increments. I prefer that approach!

More recently, as I continue to combat shame, I started leaving voice mails in the early morning when these feelings show up. I listen to them before sending. This allowed me to remember that my life was full of love even while it seemed devoid of it. I had memory and truth at the same time. Since only one can be accurate, grief then releases the memory, and healing is automatic.

There was nothing I could do to stop feeling as if I had no love or meaning. What I could do was take the step I had committed to. Talk to a co-healer. This didn't automatically bring about change. It allowed me to observe. It is my approach to healing emotionally and spiritually. This is in contrast to how I went about physical healing and detoxification. For that I went to doctors, learned what would help me feel my best, and did it. This included treatments, supplements, diet changes, and a lot of reading. It would be so nice to use this regimen with shame healing! Take nine supplements and exercise five days a week!

Chapter 15: Study the Culture

Once you have found or established a group, next is observing, as I have described. Ordinary everyday shaming is the most difficult to observe because it is integrated into the culture and seems normal. It's a special study because we have to be able to see how we are all shamed every day in order to stop receiving it.

If you print up the list of shame examples from Chapter 2, Ordinary Everyday Shaming, and have it in front of you, this kind of shaming can seem more obvious.

Television, the news, and the Internet are loaded with shaming. It is offered to those who want to shame others in order to stop their own experience of it. Notice how many times the good guys and bad guys are obvious. We get to identify with the good guys. Notice how you feel when identifying with the good guys.

Sitting with others, pause the show, and discuss the shaming you observed. If you disagree with each other, play it back and look again. Acculturated denial may make it difficult to see when shaming is right in front of you. Take your time. Remember my example of shaming, and not one person in my audiences realized I was shaming, even when I said I was giving an example of it.

You can create a practice of studying how people abuse each other, how everyone shames everyone, and how people spend time in the victim triangle. You could start with assuming that all communications and facial expressions are shaming, and then search for those that aren't! Go to a coffee shop, sit with a drink, and watch. Notice how those taking orders are feeling. What do they hide from customers, and what do they reveal? What will they gossip about when the store closes? How much shaming is in response to the person it is directed at, and how much is all the time to everyone? Is the person aware that they are putting others down, or is it habit, or rationalized?

Imagine how you would feel if you were the person you are observing. What if you were the husband with the wife impatiently tapping her foot? The person behind the Starbucks counter who asks how the customer is and gets no response? Or gets a flat, fine, thanks? How would it feel to be the mother of the child who loudly complains that he now wants a drink after the order has come? How would it feel to be that child when the mother shames him? Why has he asked for something he knows won't be given? What would you feel as one of the people you observe fighting in a restaurant with quiet voices and very serious faces? Can you imagine being the bank teller who told my client that he should have known which account to make his deposit in? What might she have been responding to? Perhaps he was playing victim, and she responded with abuser?

Watching groups of teens is informative because they shame each other and themselves in ways that are transparent. Perhaps this is because they belong to a different sub-culture, and so it is easier for adults to see than with someone in our own sub-culture. Or it may be the immaturity of their age. One of my Starbucks is next to a high school, and many students come in to sit at a large table. While they seem friendly with each other, they also put each other down, and their hierarchy is apparent.

Instead of shaming teens for their criticisms, put them in your classroom. Observe.

My colleague with step-children tries to control the TV programs they watch and proclaims the harm of shows that are based almost entirely on shaming. Frasier was based on lying and shaming, including self-shaming. The Daily Show is a good source for a new look at news, but is based largely on shaming the typical media presentations. The humor of Everyone Loves Raymond was based on the main character's response to shaming, which was seen as deserved. Even shows not based on shaming still include a great deal of it.

Study each of your environments one at a time. Begin with the least triggering, such as stores you frequent and places where you don't interact with people you know. As you approach the store, remind yourself of your task. Be prepared to study facial expressions and body language of the other shoppers and those working there. Listen to voices and sounds and tones. See if you can prove that someone isn't shaming rather than that they are! If you feel confused over whether or not someone is shaming, take someone with you and talk about it right there.

Notice people acting as if they feel shame. This may be a signal that they have been shamed. Were they? They may believe they are because of deeply internalized shame. Are they reacting, or do they always seem to feel shamed?

Observing without Language

If you have a chance to go to a country with a language you don't know, hanging out in public places listening is a great way to grasp how shaming goes on in all cultures and appears the same (allowing for cultural differences). You could also use head phones playing nonstimulating music or white sound to achieve this.

Without words to inform you, your information comes from body language, tone, facial expression, movements, and a sense of their energy. People who are shaming or feel shamed will have a hardened sense about them. They will seem to be pulled back, or pushed forward. There is no soft, flowing, smiling ease about them.

Chapter 16: Study Your Shame

First, what is your physical experience? Is it in your stomach? Skin? Throat? Do you hold your breath, taking in as little air as possible? Does your heart rate increase? Or decrease? Take a moment and check in right now. Let yourself relax, and notice all areas of your body. Then think of something that makes you feel badly about yourself. How did your body change?

Next, study the emotional experience. The emotional sensation can be more difficult to see because it is the very sensation you want to avoid. Breathing deliberately can support awareness. Call to mind something that will bring shame, but this time study your emotional reaction. How can you describe the pain? Do thoughts tend to follow? See if you can interrupt the thoughts in order to allow the emotion to flow. Breathing can assist staying with the emotion.

To heal shame we have to
feel it,
let it move around in us,
and breathe it out.

Stop Any Time

Know that you can stop this exercise. When you have had enough, use any of your methods of stopping it. You can turn to others with a comment or joke, send a text, anything to distract you from the shame. Knowing you can stop makes it easier to keep going. You have lots of time. Feeling small increments is effective.

It can be difficult to see that being depressed, waking up feeling dead, wanting to rage without knowing why, desperately wanting a drink or a drug, feeling lonely and isolated, and a long list of other symptoms are actually caused by internalized shame.

Each of us can discover how we avoid shame, and then inhibit the method for a moment or an hour or a day to see what happens. Use Chapter 6: Overriding the Experience of Shame, to create your own list of ways you avoid shame. Include anything that is common for you even if you aren't sure that you use it to avoid shame. You can determine its function later. Then, whenever you find yourself acting on one, check back to moments before and see if shame might have been trying to surface. Our favored methods are effective, and it takes some study to discover how they work.

Next you can set out to deliberately stop using one of your methods. Only one, as you don't want to invite all your shame to appear at once. This would be too much pain. The study at this point is becoming aware of your methods of avoiding it, and what it feels like if you don't.

If I still had shame when eating in restaurants by myself I could deliberately go to a restaurant, sit down, order and eat, all the while watching my shame come up. I could watch the sentences associated with it. "What's wrong with you?" "Don't have any friends?" "What are you, a loner? Some kind of alien with none of your kind here?" "No one likes you, huh?" "Well, obviously something is wrong with you. No one chooses to eat alone, do they?"

I might have answered these voices by affirming that, yes I am alone, but just because I like to be alone doesn't mean there is something wrong with me. I would watch how shame moved around in my body, and invited it to flow. I would separate this physical sensation from the emotional one, the one that pulls me down, makes me feel small, and urges me to desperately do something, anything, that will make this go away. I would ask where those voices originated. What was I still believing that made me feel shame when being alone? What is shameful about being alone?

This is easier when I deliberately tackle this life inhibitor. My shame would already be reduced because I would know that it isn't deserved, and can be healed. When I didn't know that, then all I had were the critical voices and head-shaking over how pathetic I was.

Breathing deliberately encourages the shame to flow around in you and out. Practicing yoga or Pilates can take you into your body, and breathing becomes automatic with practice. Choose the Yoga asana that allows you to drop most fully into your self. A simple roll-up will automatically expand breathing.

We inhibit breathing when we don't want to experience emotions that have made it through other barriers. If you attend your breathing when feeling any kind of distress, you can it invite it to move instead of stagnate. We can actually tolerate horrible feelings if we can discharge them.

Body workers have methods of grounding their clients to prevent that free-floating sensation that can come after body work, or when avoiding what is going on with our emotions. You may be able to ground yourself by walking. If possible walk bare footed on a lawn or dirt. Find what brings the sensation of your feet planted solidly on the ground. When shame begins to mount, see if it helps to focus attention on your feet.

Mindfulness is an approach to bring yourself into the present. Mindful meditation has been well studied as a method to settle yourself, and also reduces stress, anxiety, depression, and more. Learning how to engage the present reality serves to counterbalance the historical experiences that emerge and are now invited to be healed. Many of us have learned loving, safe present alternates to the terrifying, painful past in the service of healing. Shame is the foremost emotion that belongs in the past, and to keep it there, we must let it flow out of us by engaging our knowing of the wonderful present. Meditate mindfully even for a single minute. Inhale, hold for a few seconds, and exhale more slowly while noticing your present reality.

A client gave me a quote from *Transformations*, by Karlfried Graf von Durkheim, in which he talked about how meditation can be used to confront each new demon in order to heal it. He said not to use meditation to feel good and peaceful, and sidestep the pain, but rather to obtain the truth to heal those demons. Dr. Joe Dispenza calls it sitting in the fire.

Rules for Shame Study

There aren't any! If you notice that you are beginning to create rules about how to observe, and what to do when you see shaming, it could be because rules add order and makes sense of things. Wanting rules, or creating them, is a way to manage discomfort. It's a way to manage shame. And of course you can decide to do it.

If others create rules, and want you to follow, the answer is the same. They are merely ways to create order when there actually isn't any. Rules offer a sense of meaning and purpose and predictability that doesn't exist.

Of course you can use rules if it makes this process easier. There are no rules about not using rules, either! We get to use any and all of our defenses against shame until we don't need them any longer.

I have observed people creating a rule that one's spouse must stop shaming. This is usually applied with shaming, such as, "You're shaming me! You're not supposed to do that!"

Chapter 17: How Do You Shame Yourself?

Internalized shame becomes such a part of our identity that all people shame themselves in the ways they were shamed. Some are obvious, such as saying, "I don't know why I do that," "What's wrong with me, I can't do anything right." Another example is comparing oneself negatively to others. A friend enjoyed watching when I had my home remodeled, but expressed her admiration by comparing herself to me. I knew her reflection of my knowledge and ability was genuine, but it was offset by the comparison with which she put herself down. I wondered what childhood relationship seemed to require letting someone else win when there was actually no competition.

One victim stance is believing they have it bad while others have it better. "How did they do that? We worked hard but they have it made. What's wrong with us?"

Self-shaming is required by the culture. "I'm sorry I didn't sweep the floor." "I'm so stupid." "Now why did I do that?" "What was I thinking?" "I'm a failure." "I'm so sorry."

Self-shaming can appear as depression and anxiety. These symptoms may appear when feeling so unacceptable that belonging isn't possible. Anxiety can reflect fear that shameful qualities will be found out. Panic attacks might arise from fear that traumas occurring in childhood will occur now, but can also come from the horror of feeling the shame that accompanied them.

Believing that you don't deserve much, that you aren't entitled to love or a nice life, is shame. Humanness brings with it the right to belong in a community and develop ourselves to the fullest. No one is on the outside. Shame can interfere with knowing this. The person who feels unworthy (shame) will feel as if they are not entitled to belong. People who buy what they can't afford, or gamble compulsively, or shop addictively, or focus on wanting what they can't have are suffering from shame that prevents understanding that we all truly deserve belonging.

Self-Shaming to Avoid Shaming Others

I have observed clients and friends change the subject from how they were harmed to how they harm. Some people can't face how their mothers treated them so turn it on themselves. Self-shaming can feel less painful than taking a look at the horrors that need to be faced.

Shaming to Motivate Oneself

I mentioned the young man at the pool who actually got out, stood on the side, and berated an imaginary person in the water. Himself. People who were controlled with shame may carry this out on themselves. It's what they know, and so believe is appropriate.

Internalized Shame Is Hard to See

If I tell my friend that she is working too much and taking care of everyone else's needs to avoid feeling internalized shame, she can see me as a little crazy, and say that her job and family just require so much. It takes a lot of exploration to challenge the defense against shame and allow the truth to emerge. Once the shame about needing to be good enough drops, then she gets to understand the right way to spend time, and do it. But it means challenging the beliefs that she is only good for working hard, and she is only good for raising a family and taking care of extended family members.

Earlier I mentioned the internalized shame reflected in my alien status that prevented me from enjoying being alone. In looking back I recognize that this came from shame because of using avoidant attachment as a lifestyle.

Chapter 18: Learning to Grieve

The ability to grieve is at the top of the list of skills needed to heal shame. The anger and sadness necessary to grieve are the emotions that allow us to change our perception of life from what it once was to what it is now. When someone dies, that need is obvious. It is just as necessary when grieving past trauma and deprivation so that we can see the beauty of life.

It is said that time heals, and of course time passing does make a difference. However, when grief doesn't discharge hurts and shame, they remain in place as if they are still occurring. This can be seen in "unrequited love," where a person remains strongly bonded to the lost one. While this is romanticized as true love, it is actually the result of the lack of grief. Sadness may be felt, but isn't accompanied by necessary anger.

Our culture inhibits healthy anger and healthy crying, and the inability to grieve has left all of us with shame from childhood. If we had those emotions intact, we would have grieved it all out a long time ago. Now we can re-learn to use those tools for leaving the past in the past in order to have a full present life.

Grief has been a subject of attachment theory researchers. The first of John Bowlby's renown trilogy was called, *Attachment*; the second, *Separation: Anxiety and Anger*; and the third, *Loss: Sadness and Depression*. The titles convey the experience of grief. First, there must be an attachment to a person, or a belief, or way of life. Loss of any of these brings anger, and then sadness.

Babies angrily cry when their mother separates from them. The objective is to get her attention so she will come back. A baby's instincts tell him that if mama doesn't return, he will die because he would have, centuries ago, in the hunting and gathering days. This anger is natural to all of us when we lose something we are attached to, as our primitive brain isn't dominated by the cerebral cortex which "knows" that the person has died, or left.

As we grasp that the loss is complete, then sadness and healthy depression arrive. We are accustomed to the experience of losing someone to death by shedding tears and turning inward. This is a working depression. It helps alter reality from including that person to not including him. The more unexpected and tragic the loss, the stronger the crying and depression.

Anger and tearful letting-go alternate until resolution is complete. After that, occasional sadness comes up over time.

These emotions that release things and people important to us are the same ones that allow us to heal from hurts. When children fall down and skin knees they run to an adult and cry. When they are done, they get up and run off. But over time our culture teaches children that when they are hurt, not crying is better, and anger is not a good emotion. As a result, the very tools that allow us to be hurt and then grieve it away are impeded. It is possible to experience horrible atrocities and then cry and rage until the effects are cleaned out of us. We can leave the past in the past. First we must reclaim the right to have the emotions to do so.

Shame cannot be healed if
the emotions of anger and sadness
are not available.

Joining a group can help if you cannot grieve easily. The shame of crying, especially for men, can be eased by watching others cry with no shame. When the absurdity of holding back tears is seen for what it is, shame will dissolve. Anger can be better understood in groups, too. As members experience real anger, and how it was expressed toward them as children wasn't healthy, they can become more comfortable letting it roll out of them. Accessing emotions is a vital first step in the process of finding freedom from shame.

Physical Health Brings Productive Grief

The American Psychological Association published two books in 2004 establishing that past trauma causes physical illnesses of almost all kinds. Taking on health practices can allow grief to flow more easily, and shame-healing to increase. These practices include: detoxification, healthy diet, giving up smoking and alcohol and a long list of harmful foods, exercise and other healing approaches. It's possible that feeling better from these approaches will make it easier to tolerate discharge of shame and other results of trauma.

When Emotions Are Not Grief

Tears to Override Anger

People who aren't comfortable being angry may use tears to change anger into an emotion that feels safe. A client was talking about how horribly his father had treated him with beatings and criticism of everything he did. When I said, You're angry with him, he nodded and started crying. I told him to stop the tears and let himself have the needed anger. He talked about how when he was eighteen, he had finally punched his father to stop him from hitting his mother. He saw that I enjoyed hearing about the anger that had finally created a boundary. Then he could release the shame he felt for hitting a parent!

Anger to Override Tears

Others are comfortable with anger, but tears are frightening. Another male client could not tolerate evidence that his wife wasn't interested when she didn't give what he considers sufficient attention. Deep sadness is projected from being the child of a mother who paid no attention, but he learned to use anger to avoid the pain of it. Stopping him as I did with the first man was ineffective. I learned that if I let him be angry, and gently reach out to the hurt child several times, he would eventually tolerate some of the sadness.

Unhealthy Grief Emotions

Some crying can actually reinforce shame such as when the crying person is berating himself. This kind of crying doesn't bring relief. The grief is remorse or confession, accompanied by a sense that nothing can be done about it. It is difficult to perceive that shame is just history that needs to be grieved away.

When we professionals assess depression, we ask about tearfulness. Crying can be a symptom of depression. It is necessary to differentiate healthy, freeing grief from stagnant, clinical depression. In the second, supplements, and occasionally anti-depressants, are called for.

Grieving for Loss

Emotions when someone dies are the most familiar because it is allowed by our culture. It isn't well understood that we also grieve for other losses. When grief appears, check to see if it is for more than the circumstances. Let it come, even if people look at you strangely because your expression is over the top! Take advantage of the opportunity.

When beginning physical detoxification, I found that emotional detoxification came, too. I discovered reruns of a sitcom that brought tears because the mother was so sweetly loving to the children. Since I was grieving deprivation in my childhood, I copied every episode and watched them all twice.

More recently I took my beloved cat to the vet because he was urinating blood. Two days of antibiotics didn't help, so I took him back, only to learn that his newly diagnosed hyperthyroidism had caused weight loss and high blood pressure, which caused his retinas to detach! The vet wanted to keep him for the day to feed and hydrate him.

When the assistant came to take him from me, I started crying. I cried all the way to the parking lot, on the drive home, and the whole rest of the day.

A small portion of the tears was for my cat's poor health and his fear of staying at the vet's. Most were for enormous losses in childhood. I talked with co-healers, but didn't learn what actual loss was being grieved. I didn't care. This grief was painful because it included losing someone or something. I still welcomed it, knowing what it was doing for me.

I always welcome tears!

Grieving for Abuse

Grieving for abuse feels different, and may include body memories. Our bodies retain memory of what happened, and the sensation can emerge along with emotions. I had pain in the muscle in my upper arm that felt as if something had hit it. When I rubbed it, it hurt. I could still play racquetball, and it was gone in two days. These are indicators that it was memory, not a real injury.

This kind of grief is enjoyable because it is easy to grasp that old hurts are being cleaned out. However, if the abuses were too intense, and if shame came with them, the psychological defense mechanism of dissociation may have been employed. People can be unable to think well, wandering around the house or stores, wondering what they are doing. This is a time to call someone so that you can remember the present, and know that this is a good thing even if it feels very strange.

Grieving Out Shame

This seems to be the most difficult grief because it means feeling the shame. So while tears and anger are doing their job, the shame still feels terrible. It's necessary, though. I find that the grief feels good, but the accompanying cloudy, icky sensation that comes with it doesn't. Ask others to remind you that when it is over, you will get to discover what you healed! And that new freedoms have come.

One day I was having a wonderful time at home and in my office, seeing a few clients, writing, talking with close friends. I felt fully alive, in my life, and needing nothing more. But when my last client left I felt bad, cut off from everyone, and with no life. As I saw the contrast, I could suspect that memory emotions were coming up to be healed. When they emerge it is often hard to remember that they are not real life. After a half hour, I realized I had to call someone. I left a message with the details, and my friend called me back. I was so in the memory of being unlovable and unloved, and the avoidant attachment that accompanies that belief, that I didn't know my friend was there for me. I couldn't sense her presence, I only heard her words from a distance. It was like having a relationship, but at that moment, not believing it.

I talked about the subjects that had come up in my session, searching for a clue as to what had been triggered: my client's abuse, the shame he carried, the pain inflicted along with constant criticism by his father. This man carried much shame from his past, and from what he had done in his adult life. I felt compassion for his struggles.

And somehow, in spite of his intense shame, he was able to hear me. He recognized that I don't shame him and am here to help. He is making significant changes because of it.

I made some guesses about my own history, but nothing was clear. I watched my emotions for the rest of the evening, finally going to bed, my question unresolved.

The next morning, I started crying! It was grief at having had my love received from a friend. I told her I was here for her, and she was touched, and welcomed my caring. My love was received! Somehow that triggered the pain of deprivation of that when I was a child.

Then the session with a man who was also condemned, and could receive my caring, touched my unhealed pain. This pain could emerge to be grieved away now because after releasing so much shame, I know that I am loving and my love is received. This meant that I was crying only for childhood. None of the deprivation was happening now. My healing allowed this old experience to arise for healing, too!

This crying emerged without my understanding, and I welcomed it anyway, knowing that it would release more of the deprivation of childhood love and attachment and the accompanying shame. It felt really good because I wasn't crying for a loss. I was crying for a wonderful gain!

The following morning, I woke happy and alive to a rich day before me. It was rich not because of planned activities, but because in this present-day life, almost all of my days are rich.

Anne's Books

1. Cultivating Intuitive and Spiritual Gifts: How to Find and Develop Yours

2. Shedding Shame Workbook: Release the Cause of Depression, Anxiety, and Lack of Self Care
        Companion to Shedding Shame
        and Claiming Freedom

3. Growing Up Hated: A Memoir of Shedding Shame

4. Jesus and Shame: The Shame That Forgiveness Cannot Relieve

5. Reclaiming Healthy Sexual Energy: Revised